Inside the Faculty Union

Inside the Faculty Union

Labor Relations in the University Setting

Robert Engvall

ROWMAN & LITTLEFIELD
Lanham • Boulder • New York • London

Published by Rowman & Littlefield
An imprint of The Rowman & Littlefield Publishing Group, Inc.
4501 Forbes Boulevard, Suite 200, Lanham, Maryland 20706
www.rowman.com

Unit A, Whitacre Mews, 26-34 Stannary Street, London SE11 4AB

British Library Cataloguing in Publication Information Available

Library of Congress Cataloging-in-Publication Data Available

ISBN 978-1-4758-4507-5 (cloth : alk. paper)
ISBN 978-1-4758-4508-2 (pbk. : alk. paper)
ISBN 978-1-4758-4509-9 (electronic)

Contents

Acknowledgments

So many to thank, so little space in which to do it. First, my wife, Janet, who provides constant support and believes in me beyond any rational measure. The experience of leading one's colleagues in an academic union requires constant support, and without her, I'd have never regained my sense of self or my sense of humor. I'm reluctant to thank individual colleagues, for inevitably some will be left out, but I must thank Lisa Newcity and Melissa Russano for their tireless work on behalf of the union during my presidency. Their efforts weren't always rewarded, and no amount of good work or good judgment could ultimately save them from being tainted by my own failings, but they tried. They really, really tried, and for that, I'm grateful. Our friendship survived some amazing trials and tribulations, and lesser friends would have walked away from me during the process.

Finally, without the belief in this project by my editor, Tom Koerner, there would be nothing here to acknowledge. Without his guiding hand and willingness to see this story make it to print, I'd still be talking to myself about all of this, and frankly, that simply couldn't be healthy. Last and certainly not least, Emily Tuttle, whose assistance in keeping this project moving forward, at Tom's direction, actually did move this project forward. Her patience and kindness throughout the project did not go unnoticed and shouldn't go unacknowledged.

Introduction

There's no way of knowing why you hold this book in your hands. Even if it may simply be a mistake or an oversight, now that you are looking at it, you might find a book that could appeal to both professors and administrators in equal measure, though perhaps with differing reviews of the content.

Faculty members may be interested to hear what really happens inside the faculty union and what union presidents do day to day. Administrators might be interested to know how faculty union leaders may view their relationships with those above them and how that affects the university generally. Others outside of those two realms but who remain interested in higher education and what is happening in labor relations among the various participants may also have more than a passing interest.

If you begin this book with the mindset that unions are in great peril, particularly as they apply to higher education, it's likely that you may find support in these pages for that belief. If you begin this book looking to buoy your belief that higher education needs unionism to improve the working conditions of those on campus and, ultimately the product produced, you will at least find that you may not be alone.

There are no guarantees that you will feel better about the state of higher education and the interplay of the union and the administration after reading this book, but you will, hopefully, gain a more nuanced understanding of that relationship. Perhaps that can be a starting point for a better understanding of where we are and where we, in theory, all want to be.

If you had a nickel for every introduction read over the years suggesting that the book about to be read was written because the author hadn't seen anything like it before, you'd have a lot of nickels. Having said that, this book was written because there really hasn't been anything quite like it, and therefore, much of what is said in the following pages, really needed to be said. A book about "labor relations in the university setting" ideally will assist those who might read it in more fully understanding the realities surrounding the many contentious issues that are part of adversarial relationships in the "professional" setting of a college campus.

Most of the multiple experiences that occur during one's own union presidency tend, with the passage of time, to become less painful and more amusing than they probably were at the time of their occurrence. As a result, there becomes a greater ability to more objectively draw upon those many experiences to expose some of the dynamics that both underlie and often undermine academic life.

This is a book about what happens in higher education from the perspective of one who has served and written from memory, from contemporaneous notes taken memorializing significant events, and from a somewhat biased account of those events. Search as you might, you won't be able to locate contemporaneous newspaper accounts verifying or disputing the claims about to be made.

There could be some toes that get stepped on and some feelings that would appropriately be hurt were the actors depicted shrewd enough to recognize themselves in the stories told. Some will undoubtedly be that perceptive; many others will not. But that's another dead horse to be beaten some more later. For now, suffice it to say that the events described in the following pages are real and the readers of these events as depicted will gain knowledge from fully understanding these stories and either seeing themselves or others they know in them. Both sides, labor and management, are depicted, though there can be little argument that one side is more favorably depicted than the other. Some people might disagree entirely that any of this truly needs to be said. Many union presidents probably simply leave well enough alone and repress as many of these memories as they can. That is their right, and it's possible they're right.

Everyone could write a book about what has happened in their work lives and how those things could benefit others similarly situated in the future. But apparently, not everyone has the time or inclination to write such a book. I have and I did, and this is how it begins.

Chapter One

There Is But One Truth, but That Truth May Not Be Enough

The Foundation of Labor Relations in the University Setting

Let's begin at the true beginning: we understand the past based on how somebody who was there relates the story and moves it forward. As the past becomes more removed, so do the stories. Just as when small children played "telephone" and we recognized that stories passed from one to another tended to change along the way, so too do the stories that we adults relay to and from one to another.

The credibility of those from whom we get our stories determines what level of credence we give those stories. We should probably believe contemporaneous *New York Times* accounts of historical events more than we should believe the memories of our grandfathers, but then again, sometimes grandpa had it mostly right too. We add it all up, and we get what seems appropriate to believe.

You simply need to add it all up and put it all together and draw whatever conclusions you see fit concerning unionism in higher education and how the stories woven together here either confirm your suspicions and existing knowledge or challenge your present worldview. Either way, your own truths may very well be challenged, and your own perceptions may, in some cases at least, actually be altered.

The stories you are about to read, the thoughts expressed, and the lessons (hopefully) learned, should have wide appeal and are intended to let you in on some of the dirty little secrets that encompass much of academia today (at least unionized academia). Exposing those secrets is far larger and more important than the role that any individual may play in how those secrets play out and continue to play out on university campuses.

Although the experiences shared herein are very real, they may not be universal. Still, they can be useful to those of you finding yourselves in the role of a faculty leader, a negotiator, an administrator, or even someone with a passing interest in how these mostly unseen and behind-the-scenes happenings actually happen.

Every effort will be made to allow the description of these experiences to assist you in universalizing them and using them in your own work lives as best you can. What would you have done if you were in the position of union leader, and/or how might you have done things differently should be ever-present questions in the back of your mind as you turn these pages.

"We understand the past from the words of those who experienced it."
(Klosterman, 2016, pp. 153–154)

This book is sometimes depressing, sometimes angry, and sometimes hopeful, all of which parallel the life of a union leader in the university setting. The truth is, too many of us have found that our experiences have forced us to either care too much about things seemingly out of our control or to care too little about things perfectly within our control. Union leaders struggle mightily trying to find the proper mix, and many leave their positions wondering whether finding it is even possible.

You don't have to be David Byrne of the Talking Heads to wake up one day and wonder aloud "How did I get here?" In truth, you can be a rather run-of-the-mill college professor going about your business who then discovers yourself in a place in which every day begins with the same sentiment: "How did I get here?" and "Is there an exit?"

There is a fair amount of disdain in these pages for those in authority. That disdain is the inevitable result of union leadership, and a fair assessment of labor relations in the university setting probably requires an acknowledgment of the role that both sides, labor and management, play in creating that mindset.

Proportioning the proper amount of blame and credit for events that happen in the university setting is difficult. Making a determination of what persons or which parties may be mostly to blame for various disasters probably cannot be done without a degree of bias and preconceived notions creeping into the mix. There will be every effort made to acknowledge that bias where it exists or at least to recognize places where it may.

Ultimately, it will largely be up to you to determine in given circumstances how that blame should be dispensed. Does it lie mostly with the faculty and union leadership as being the direct result of the incompetence of the various players involved on the faculty side? Or in contrast, is it more the result of the many beacons of ineffectualness who lord their many powers over individual faculty members and over the faculty as a whole? Either way, there will likely be plenty of blame to be thrown around.

The only real point of determining who is to blame, beyond whatever level of personal satisfaction there may be in a given moment, is to determine how best not to repeat mistakes already made. The main point of this writing is to assist you in figuring out ways not to repeat the mistakes of the past and how to chart a course toward a better future in which union leaders and administrators might somehow become more productive university collaborators.

The truth is, academic life offers a series of contradictions. To suggest that most of us have seen the good, the bad, and the ugly isn't merely cliché; it's actually true. We have seen arrogance and humility. We have seen expertise and incompetence. This book hopes to impart wisdom gained through the years and in the role of union president. To that end, each chapter will feature a summary titled "Lessons Learned" in an attempt to relatively briefly encapsulate what was learned through the experience and thus what you might learn from the retelling of the story.

It would be folly to think that there couldn't be another version or even perhaps more than one other version of the history about to be shared in the following pages and chapters. This is the story of labor relations in the university setting from the vantage point of the leader of the labor side of the equation, and if somebody from the administration or from any administration wants to tell their story their way, they are more than welcome to do so.

Until that happens, this will be the best record of the events of a union presidency through the eyes of the union president himself. More generally, it may serve as an accounting, less of the individual experiences of a union president, but more as the experience of what surely must be common to many union presidencies. As such, this might serve as useful experience for those involved in this sort of thing from a variety of perspectives.

You are encouraged to put yourself in the shoes of the union president as often as you can and question that version of the story along the way as you see fit. Most importantly, as you put yourself in those shoes, imagining the competing interests and internal conflicts, we can all find hope and optimism that if you find yourself in these situations, you can learn from the experiences herein.

Spending a few years as union president is definitely spending time away from what could be time better spent and involves coming to terms with living in the kind of intellectual desert that leaves one parched and thirsting for release. Any release.

It's a wonder that no crimes were committed. Some were considered. It's a wonder that those who do this kind of work remain gainfully, if all too often, ineffectually employed. It's a wonder that we might have any friends remaining given what tends to be a multiyear sentence that involves significant doses of self-pity, confusion, and general miserableness.

You may find this writing to be a letter to all of our younger selves, or perhaps your still-young selves, who remain able and willing to make a positive impact upon your organization. It is also a letter to those contemplating life in academia or those already in academia considering becoming more involved; it is, in sum, a cautionary tale.

Go ahead and do what you feel you have to do, run for a union position or become active in your local academic union; just go in with your eyes open. Your involvement may very well not make your professional life better, and it is entirely possible, if not probable, that it will make it infinitely worse. Even more frightening, the emotional trauma you may endure may take a toll personally; so if your family and support system won't be with you no matter how miserable you might get, then forget about it, keep on walking, don't turn around, don't look back, and don't answer the call to serve as a union leader.

This book adds a genuinely new and hopefully helpful perspective to the topic of labor relations in the university setting, a perspective that many probably have but few have openly shared. Along the way, you may also find some genuine sorrow and anger expressed, although somewhat tempered by humor, and most of all, a recognition that although this is a serious issue, taking ourselves too seriously as we confront the many absurdities we face can be counterproductive to our work lives and our personal health.

If you assume the position of union leader, your experiences will likely be similar to those you will read about in the chapters to follow. In as much, assuming that position will mean that there will also be moments when you may be inclined to also assume the fetal position. You may lose your sense of humor for a while as daunting problems mount and the pressures you face at times seem insurmountable. But on the upside, your sense of humor will probably return.

More globally, or at least more grandly, this book also explores the larger competing questions of whether unionism is compatible with higher education generally or whether the increasing corporatization of the university makes unionism more important than ever. These questions are open to debate, and either view may, at least much of the time, be purely rational. Leading such a union, however, is entirely irrational and is the type of life choice that should make one question his or her very ability to make any life choices at all.

The position of union president in the university setting is unlikely to offer many tangible rewards. Most who do this work do it either entirely voluntarily or for very little compensation. It is truly a mission done to improve the lot of your coworkers and done for the "love of the union" rather than to advance any personal or financial interest.

There tends to be infinitely more sorrow and pain than humor and gladness, though there are parts of each within a description of both the day-to-day realities of being union president and the soul-crushing experience of negotiating a contract with a university administration. If ever there were a more David and Goliath encounter than a unionized faculty negotiating against professional negotiators on the administration's side, it is difficult to conceive of.

There is real pain involved in failing miserably almost every time. It can be perceived not only as good versus evil, but it generally involves a ragtag group of selected professors hoping against hope to hold on to what they had always had, negotiating against an experienced legal team and administration whose priority number one is to reach a favorable contract on their terms.

Those terms may very well include such things as decreasing university contributions to retirement, increasing faculty contributions to health care, and generally diminishing any perceived or real power or status that faculty members might have. A faculty negotiating team's priorities also include maintaining their sanity while negotiating at the same time they teach, advise, research, and generally do all those professor-type things that professors do. Although many university administrators may suspect that those "mundane" things are almost completely devoid of any real value, they are things that nevertheless occupy faculty members and take up at least forty hours of a typical workweek.

In essence, a faculty negotiating team has two full-time jobs—the work for which they were hired and the work involved in negotiating—whereas the administration is largely free to schedule around whatever it is that administrators do. Most of us could never be entirely certain of what it was that most of the administrators were doing, but we did recognize that there seemed to be a constant need for more of them.

If your university is like most, then you too have probably noticed an increase in the number of administrative positions all around you, and it's not always immediately apparent why they are there. At least we know when a faculty member is hired that he or she will engage in teaching, research, and service and that students will fill their classrooms and their offices when they are in need of recommendations or counsel. As for administrators, the definition of their duties is not always so clear.

The opportunity to morph from a respected professor in good standing, seemingly admired by one's peers and even the administration, into a pariah, at least moderately loathed by many faculty peers and largely despised by formerly friendly administrators, is a future that awaits many who undertake the role of union president. Maintaining the friendships that you have and only damaging the ones on the periphery is certainly possible if you manage things effectively, but serving in this role without doing lasting damage to some relationships is simply not possible.

Advocating for faculty interests within the adversarial nature of union/management negotiations cannot always be a gentle process. Feelings will get hurt, relationships will suffer, and knowing that before you take this position is vital to effectively dealing with those realities when they occur.

High hopes will likely give way to low expectations, and promises will frequently give way to apologies. All in all, it can be a pretty miserable experience. That said, there will probably be moments of humor and good cheer and friendships forged in the foxhole just as surely as enemies will be created.

Perhaps most of all, this book illustrates the seriousness of the topic of collective negotiations and unionism in a "professional" environment as it is juxtaposed with the absurdity of speaking on behalf of a disparate group of individuals who see themselves as almost entirely independent. This absurdity is also illustrated by the simple reality that this is written by a college professor who now speaks in terms of "enemies" and "foxholes." Most of us who assume these positions don't really see that coming.

The expression "herding cats" wasn't invented to describe a college faculty, but it certainly could've been. Faculty members are an agenda-driven group for sure, but unfortunately, that involves dozens of agendas, many of which are entirely incompatible with those held by others.

Imagine a scenario in which many individual faculty members want smaller course loads so they can focus on their research agendas, whereas other faculty members with little or no interest in research fear what that would mean for their futures; other faculty members may be concerned about their family health-care plans and parental leave policies, whereas others view all of that as far less important than retirement benefits.

One might be hard pressed to find a place with more disparate yet "educated" views than a university campus. Some of those views may be hard to endure, such as the few faculty members on your campus who are so hell-bent on sustainability issues that they might question the morality of those who bring children into the world. That is but one example of folks who might see policies such as parental leave or improvements to a family medical plan through radically different lenses than other, more traditionally minded faculty members.

Unlike many workplaces, university workplaces are filled with faculty members who are usually open about their opinions (at least with other faculty members and almost certainly with their union leaders). Some of those opinions pit faculty with children in different places from faculty members without or faculty members on the cusp of retirement in different places from those just beginning their careers. Although that is no doubt true of every unionized workplace, on a university campus, the divides among the workers somehow seem more pronounced.

At many universities, research requirements and the agenda of the administration change over the years, while older faculty may be reluctant or unable to change with that agenda. Beyond that, it may simply be a matter of equity that older professors, hired under terms in which teaching was paramount and research secondary, might now find themselves in a changing environment with younger professors pushing them out and devaluing their service.

Bringing these parties together can be difficult, but doing so, at least in part, is critical to maintaining union unity. Any rips in the fabric of union solidarity will be quickly exploited by an administration eager to pit one group of faculty members against another. If perhaps the faculty union won't technically be broken, it can nevertheless be so badly fractured that its already limited power becomes diminished even more.

The absurdity that, in many cases, is academia, is played out via the very different lens of a faculty union presidency. We've heard about university happenings from the perspective of faculty presidents and faculty members, but seldom have we heard about university happenings from the perspective of the union president. Perhaps that is because it's often too difficult for the union president to share his or her thoughts without betraying confidences or otherwise compromising the union. In this moment of increased corporatization within academia, it may not be overly dramatic to suggest that the future of academic unionization may depend on an inside look at labor relations in the university setting.

Something that has been shrouded in darkness for too long needs a bit of the disinfectant that sunlight can provide. The following chapters, it is hoped, provide at least a glimpse of that light.

LESSONS LEARNED

Unions in higher education are on the ropes. Although that most certainly is not your fault, you nonetheless should be aware that if you choose to involve yourself in union activism, you will almost assuredly be on the defensive in short order. The corporatization of higher education is in full swing, and whatever countervailing forces there may be out there, including faculty unions, the reality is that those forces are on their heels.

As a union leader you will need to somehow marshal the strength of the collective in your little slice of the world in a way that many of us before you have struggled to do. Your administration will probably do a great job of providing your union membership with a "common enemy" to fight. If the psychology is correct and having a common enemy tends to bring people closer together, then you will likely need to seize upon that.

Ideally, it would seem as though coming together for a common cause would be the natural result of the adversarial relationship between a unionized faculty and its administration. You might hope, as we all might hope, that "justice" and appropriate compromise will ultimately be the result of two sort-of equal parties fighting it out and putting all their cards on the table.

To make that dream resemble reality, at least in some form, you have to keep your collective, collective. If you cannot bring people together based on their common interests and you find that their disparate beliefs are simply too great, you will be forced to tap in to their baser instincts of fighting a common enemy. It would be nice if that weren't necessary, but it would be malpractice on behalf of your members not to recognize that it may very well be necessary.

REFERENCE

Klosterman, C. (2016). *But What If We're Wrong: Thinking about the Present as If It Were the Past*. New York: Blue Rider Press.

Chapter Two

Journey to the Center of the Worst

For the person in the position of union president, it is the best of times, and it is the worst of times. Mostly though, it is the worst of times. If union presidents are mostly to blame for their many predicaments, there are nevertheless many to thank for the various influences that ultimately get them through and who hopefully will assist them in maintaining their relative sanity. For me, the former union president who writes this, beyond the usual credits that thank family and friends and lament the long hours spent and the family time missed, there are too many literary influences to even begin to mention . . . but one in particular warrants an immediate mention.

A relatively current book that might perhaps influence the mindset of a current union leader and certainly influenced me is Tom Nichols's *The Death of Expertise: The Campaign against Established Knowledge and Why It Matters*. The title likely speaks for itself; the gist of the book indeed laments much of society's seeming abandonment of expertise and wisdom in favor of some sort of raw and uneducated populism.

Many of our political leaders, of both major parties, quite ably represent the now horrifying adage that "truly, anyone can grow up to be president." It is not, unfortunately, difficult to imagine how many other people of authority have gained their positions of authority without having much to offer in the way of helping the cause of the organization over which they hold some influence and power. Most of us in academia have probably been witness to some great academic minds and leaders, but sadly and in truth, we've also been witness to many more who simply don't fit any description quite so well as "ineffectual."

Although we certainly wouldn't want our surgeons or our airline pilots to abandon their education and their experience, we seem to hold no such standard for many of our leaders, and perhaps most obviously, our political class seems ever more to be an absolute study in anti-intellectualism—the less you know, the less you want to know, the more qualified you seem to be. It is madness, and yet it is played out more frequently than ever before.

Nichols, however, didn't take nearly as negative a view of all this as some might. Despite his concerns about the death of expertise as a phenomenon, he seemed to be somewhat hopeful that in most cases, we simply couldn't survive this way and thus we'd eventually find it in ourselves to value expertise again. His glass-half-full notion suggested that we societally would change this disturbing and relatively newfound desire to denigrate knowledge and exalt the uninformed.

In contrast, many of us more prone to hold the glass-half-empty view worry that we just won't get over the tendency to denigrate the informed or that even a mass of educated people would be unable to overcome a lesser mass of louder (by nature) and uninformed people bent on hating the educated and "elite," which seemed to come to mean the same thing in many circles.

Nichols remained hopeful that separating the credentialed from the incompetent would be assisted by experience. He seemed to believe experience would win out. Most of us, most surely, hope he's correct.

Eventually, "bad teachers over time will tend to get bad evaluations, lousy lawyers will lose clients, and untalented athletes will fail to make the cut" (Nichols, 2017, p. 33). True, and yet bad politicians get reelected again and again, bad business leaders make fortunes, and bad university administrators hire more bad administrators to badly administer in the same way they have done.

All of which seems to make perfect sense as long as you don't think about it too much. Which, by the way, would make an excellent title for a book, perhaps even this one: *This Makes Perfect Sense as Long as You Don't Think about It Too Much*. Think about all the meetings you've attended and all the initiatives that have been rolled out that only made sense if you refused to think about them too much. It boggles the academic mind.

Think about all the bad policies and/or the poor administration of those policies that require some type of cleanup. Much of it seems to represent a genuine death of expertise in favor of the rebirth of the celebration of rank amateurism.

Not everyone survives the many trials by fire that most professionals endure, but most of those who truly survive, according to Nichols, have some level of expertise that has assisted them well in the process. Even if not all of us are as committed to the "cream rises to the top" notion as Nichols, and many others may be, we should continue to hope for the best. This hope, however, doesn't lessen our collective need to prepare for the worst.

Preparing for the worst is a necessary requirement for a university union leader, a position in which competence is vital, of course, but in which more than competence is required. This is especially true in an environment in which far too many seem far too ready to believe the worst about those on their side and accept the best about those who most assuredly are not.

As it turns out, neither likeability nor trustworthiness matter as much as you'd think they might or you'd think they should. Being an unlikeable and dishonest reprobate may in reality actually make for a more effective union president.

If you are hung up on the stubbornness of facts and the need to have your constituency treated with a certain level of dignity, the role of union leader may not be for you. These things, it turns out, really don't matter that much anymore, at least when it comes to negotiating a contract with a university administration. Universities are much closer to corporations than they are families, and as a result many of the human relationships that used to matter so much seem to matter less all the time.

Our "fact-free" political environment in which nothing seems to matter anymore—punch a reporter, get elected anyway; cheat on your several spouses, get elected anyway; lie about major issues, get elected anyway—seemed to be already present in negotiations between faculty and administration. As a precursor to this line of reasoning, a union president must immediately come to accept and figure out how to deal with two competing narratives. Many, if not most, universities have two very effective competing narratives that largely go unchallenged.

When speaking to faculty and staff, the administration tends to assure them that enrollments are tenuous, that trouble is always just over the horizon, and that sacrifice must be the order of the day to ensure survival for all. These are tough times for higher education, after all.

In contrast, when administrators speak to those on the outside, like parents, trustees, and the general public, the future tends to be nothing but blindingly bright. New buildings are being built on nearly every college campus, new programs are continually initiated, and the future is limited only by those who don't recognize limitless potential.

Bridging this gap may prove far more difficult than you might think it would be. After all, how could you go public with what you know when putting forth that information might actually lead to declining enrollments and a less brilliant future? Undercutting the publicly accepted narrative seems almost treasonous, and perhaps more importantly, it seems as though it would threaten the long-term prospects of every faculty member. There is a very fine line between being a sellout to the corporate and public line and selling oneself and one's peers out to a future of decreased enrollments and all the many pains that are associated with that particular outcome.

Some level of self-preservation requires that faculty members accede (at least publicly) to the "rose-colored" stories that administrations tend to tell the public. It will be difficult for you to simultaneously accept the administration's public narrative and fight that same narrative behind closed doors, and yet you are almost required to do so.

If faculty members diminish their own universities publicly, then they might very well find themselves in a place with declining enrollments, declining donations, and declining prospects for all involved. Although it may seem that a union leader could hold an administration's feet to the fire by threatening to expose and contrast their public positions with their private positions, it may very well be academic suicide to do so.

The truth, in truth, didn't really matter. It was perception above all else, and that nugget of painful reality will almost certainly be hurled in your negotiating team's direction on an almost daily basis, the true death of expertise and established knowledge in favor of perception and what can be sold most effectively.

The basic premise of *The Professionalization of Teaching* (1999), published more than twenty years ago, was that we (societally) needed to improve the lot of teachers, at all levels of education. We needed to treat them with more respect, pay them better, and generally professionalize the vocation of teaching.

It seemed like a good idea at the time; in fact it seemed almost inarguable. But like many of our deepest thoughts, the notion wasn't really advanced very effectively by either myself or others. It's probably true that most of us eventually come to accept that perhaps most of our deepest thoughts aren't as worthwhile as we'd like them to be, but that acceptance doesn't mean we have to entirely give up thinking that our next idea could be the one with lasting merit.

Maybe advancing the idea that teachers needed to be afforded more respect was neither original nor practical, but it was, nevertheless, hopeful. Especially for those of us so committed to the profession. Much of that hope, so many years later, seems all but dashed, and the role that unions were supposed to play in improving that status seems very much in doubt.

Now, authors such as Berube and Ruth (2015) speak of the "de-professionalization of teaching." They lament it, of course, just as we all probably do, but nevertheless, they speak of it openly and with the begrudging reality that suggests it is a very real thing constituting a very real threat to a once proud profession. They have seen the future, and the future for teaching as a profession is not entirely bright.

Teaching, at all levels, including higher education, suffers through some outrageous criticisms and negative stereotypes, and some of those arrows hit their mark, inflicting wounds ranging from mere scratches to those that require far more attention. One of those wounds ever more inflicted upon higher education faculty involves the diminishment of respect for the profession itself, which often ends in the lessening of the protections of tenure and the abandonment of the tenure track itself.

Teaching should be valued more than it is, and teachers at all levels should garner more respect than they do. But the truth is, they mostly don't. "Those who can, do; and those who can't, teach" is a stinging criticism, and an inaccurate one to boot, but nevertheless it is powerful and commonly held. Perhaps it's because most everyone along the way has been subjected to a bad teacher, and they tend to remember it.

Whatever level of truth attaches to the perceptions of teachers, the general and ongoing diminishment of the profession tends to harm the bargaining strength of those who fight on their behalf. Teaching is far more important in our national rhetoric than it is in our national perception. Similarly, it is far more important in the rhetoric of our university administrators (particularly when parents are around) than it is actually perceived.

All of which suggests that the past twenty years for many of us in the teaching profession have been as passengers on a rather demoralizing and diminishing journey, a journey to the center of all that is discouraging in higher education: administrative fiat, shared governance in rhetoric only, and a race to the bottom of the pay scale, all without the protection of tenure. It is, it appears, a journey to the center of the worst.

LESSONS LEARNED

It will be tempting to speak the truth to the outside world. Any union leader will feel, at one time or another, an almost overpowering need to "go public" and tell the world how dishonest the administration is being and how disconnected their rhetoric is from their actions. Unfortunately, doing so, even if satisfying in the short term, would likely result in negative long-term consequences for the university as a whole and the faculty as a major player in that whole.

Somehow, you must overcome that temptation and focus on building the status of the faculty rather than tearing down the credibility of the administration, at least publicly. You should promote with all your ability the good things that your faculty members are doing and the value they are bringing to the university. In doing so, you will both appropriately ingratiate yourself with your own membership and help unify the faculty for the hard road ahead. Any political capital you can build with your own membership will be spent down the road, and the more you can build, the more you can spend when you need it, and you'll almost certainly need it.

There is another way, but it is potentially dangerous and should only be the method of last resort. You might consider this the "loose cannon" approach, to be taken only in dire circumstances.

As a loose cannon, you might be able to put fear into the hearts and minds of administrators. Even though they know, as suggested in this chapter, that going public would potentially be suicidal for the faculty, they nevertheless really don't want you to do that. After all, their reputations as truth tellers and their credibility would be on the line.

Perhaps even their board of trustees would be appalled to know of their duplicity, or if not that, their inability to hold their faculty in line. Either way, it might be enough of a loss for the administration that they would be unwilling to call your bluff. It's risky business and probably cannot be condoned . . . unless it's your only hope. In which case, you didn't hear it here.

REFERENCES

Berube, M. & Ruth, J. (2015). *The Humanities, Higher Education, and Academic Freedom.* New York: Palgrave Macmillan.

Engvall, R. (1997). *The Professionalization of Teaching: Is It Truly Much Ado about Nothing?* Lanham, MD: University Press of America.

Nichols, T. (2017). *The Death of Expertise: The Campaign against Established Knowledge and Why It Matters.* New York: Oxford University Press.

Chapter Three

The Great and Widening Divide

Increased dependence on non-tenure-track faculty and contingent staff seems to allow for the flexibility that ever more corporatized administrations so openly desire. The subsequent overuse of adjuncts becomes a divisive issue in the academy, perhaps just as administrators imagined it might be.

Dividing full-timers from part-timers seems yet another effective way to weaken all of us. Adjuncts, our greatest heroes in many ways, for all the dirty work they do for low pay, lower benefits, and zero glory, are also sadly our worst enemies, as the "adjunctification" of the professoriate and the death of tenure run hand in hand. The overreliance upon adjunct faculty members at so many of our universities continues to get worse, and how union leaders respond to that overreliance is among their biggest worries.

If we work to improve the treatment of adjuncts, will we then be "normalizing" the hyper-dependence upon adjuncts and contributing to the death of the tenure track? If we do not work to improve the treatment of adjuncts, are we throwing good, hard-working people to the wolves in pursuit of our own self-interests? It is a genuine catch-22, a genuine "damned if we do, damned if we don't" scenario.

Increasing use of adjuncts at the expense of tenure-track lines leads to certain inevitable outcomes. One of these outcomes in play at most institutions today happens when the administration works long and hard to sell the concept of and then installs "lecturers."

Lecturers are, or would be, a group of people working under limited-term contracts doing the teaching work that tenured professors used to do. The length of the contract might vary, ranging from two years at some universities to perhaps three or even four years at many others. Despite the length of the term, one thing would be certain: the contract would not be open-ended; it would involve a set term.

This meant that although "contract professors" or lecturers would not be as hopelessly contingent as adjuncts, they would nevertheless resemble adjuncts far more than they would resemble tenured professors. Knowing that they had but a few short years to prove themselves and working for half the salary or so of more traditional tenured professors, they surely would have academic freedom only as far as that freedom provided for pleasing the administrators in charge of their renewals.

A different world it would be, that's for sure, and one in which a more "flexible workforce" would become present on college campuses. Maybe it won't contribute to the death of the profession as many of us believe it will, but it certainly will contribute to radical changes in the profession of college teaching. It's a change that also suggests that in the past twenty years any hopes for greater professionalization have given way to just trying to stem the tide of greater "de-professionalization."

From the perspective of a union president, it seems so obvious as to barely warrant an explanation that faculty members should oppose the notion of lecturers at the expense of tenure-track faculty. Better minds than mine have failed in figuring out why some people simply cannot be made to understand what seems so obvious to the rest of us. The explanation shouldn't be so difficult: in sum, the administration wants to save money, and tenure-track professors make more money and have more job security than lecturers do.

The administration wants to get lecturers into the mix because of what they perceive to be (or at least what they sell as) a necessary cost-saving measure. This should make it obvious that the intent of the administration, any administration, is *not* to suddenly replace adjuncts with lecturers and pay them a higher wage for the betterment of the university.

The intent of the administration is to replace full-time (tenure-track) faculty with full-time faculty (lecturers) making far less money. Thus, the ratio of full-time to part-time will remain socially acceptable and acceptable to accrediting bodies while far less tenure-track faculty will actually exist. This "replacement" will not happen overnight, and it may be subtle enough to go unnoticed by many, at least for a while and at least until the process of hiring lecturers over tenure-track appointments is firmly in place.

Tenure will likely protect those of us who remain, but as retirements occur, lecturers will replace many of the formerly tenured professors. That seems easy to understand, and rest assured that the administration understands it and it is why those in leadership positions tend to oppose it so vigorously.

Many of you reading this are already at places where lecturers have made inroads into the tenure track, and the rest of you are probably at places where your administration is thinking about it. They've been thinking about it for a long time, and it's been the natural evolution of thinking about ways to eliminate tenure. If hyper-dependence upon adjuncts is the new normal, then increased dependence upon lecturers will become the next normal.

If tenure cannot be eliminated overnight, it can be weakened to such an extent that eventually there will be too few tenure-track faculty to wield much influence. It may take some time; it may even take more time than many administrations had envisioned, but eventually, without resistance, it will almost surely happen.

Unfortunately, it may very well happen even with resistance, but resistance in this case is not futile, for at the very least, it will slow the inexorable slide toward a more contingent workforce in the university. Slowing that slide is in the best interests of all the many citizens within the university community, not least of all the students, whose relationships with their full-time tenure-track professors is at the heart of the very best educational outcomes.

It's not as if we should necessarily think of these attempts to weaken tenure as some sort of evil that we cannot understand. After all, any employer in a perfect world would love to have a flexible workforce in which "bad" employees can be removed and "good" employees can be empowered. The problem, of course, lies in the vast difference between the perfect world and what actually exists in the world in which we live.

But as if we were discussing religion or politics, any reasonable discussion of this seems to break down almost immediately, and passion overtakes reason with a small but vocal minority. At some universities, there are particularly vocal adjunct instructors who seem to believe, against all reason, evidence, and logic, that adjuncts will become lecturers and they'll all be making more money.

Some adjuncts seem personally convinced that when lecturers are installed, many of those who become lecturers will be long-suffering adjuncts and suddenly they will double (or more) their salaries and their lives will be vastly improved. Given this mindset, it seems perfectly understandable why passions and even anger might be stirred, for after all, why would the union be fighting the advancement of its adjunct members?

Union leaders face a very serious communications battle on this front, but they must make clear to the membership that increasing the use of lecturers is not meant to decrease the use of adjuncts but rather to decrease the use of tenure-track positions. Many university administrations now seek full-time and yet contingent workforces because it seems to play better to accreditors and to the public than the advanced use of part-time contingent workforces. Fighting the good fight for the continued and even the expanded use of full-time tenure-track workforces at our universities is where the rubber meets the road for union leaders.

The reality, of course, is that the union doesn't fight the advancement of its adjuncts, but union leadership must do its best to protect tenure and the competitive wages, hours, and working conditions of the majority of faculty and the very concept of tenure and "full-time" noncontingent faculty. It's hard to imagine that many adjunct professors would actually believe that any administration would simply want to pay its many adjuncts far more than they presently make. But perhaps, given the difficulties and insecurities that are inherent in being an adjunct professor, it is to be understood that any hope is better than the seeming hopelessness of many of their working conditions.

Union leaders must accept and do their best to deal with arguments in which passion seems to overtake reason. It may be as simple as the fact that people often hear what they want to hear.

It's difficult to be certain why the rush to diminish the professoriate seems to be such a unified desire on the part of administrators on campuses far and wide. It doesn't seem to be smart policy. In fact, researchers have shown repeatedly that when people feel mistreated and dissatisfied with their jobs, they are unwilling to do extra work to help their organizations, to expend "discretionary effort" (Sutton, 2007, pp. 40–41). Why, in the face of contradictory research, amplified by common sense, this workplace reality is completely lost on so many of our employers (and possibly yours) remains a mystery.

It likewise remains a mystery why clearly incompetent administrators often last for years doing clearly incompetent work. After all, they don't even have tenure. What they do have is something even more powerful, the built-in networking protections that they allow each other—a critically important and powerful bond that allows each administrator to accept what other administrators produce or fail to produce.

At many universities, it allows administrator after administrator to propose changes, study those changes, study them some more, and then ultimately abandon them entirely. This process, as you might imagine, can take years.

But what can take even longer is when the process starts over and then over again. A committee is often formed; an issue is studied; proposals are put forth; and then, either because the powers that be disagree with the proposals or never intended to implement any of them anyway, nothing happens. Truly, nothing happens—until a few years pass and someone intemperately brings up the work of that mysterious and now dead committee and there becomes a need to create an entirely new committee comprised entirely of new people unencumbered by any institutional history that might have them question or revisit or use any previous work. It seems to take many administrators to keep this circular system moving along.

There are many mysteries present in higher education. Primarily, why do faculty and administrations so often have such disparate goals and contradictory paths toward achieving what those outside of academia might see as fairly simple missions: to educate the students who come before them? Why, given all of that, can't we all just get along?

Given our disparate views and interests, it may become understandable why faculty and administration often become oil and water, but what is more difficult to comprehend is why it is so difficult for faculty members to support and unite with other faculty members. Distrust runs deep.

Some administrations take full advantage of their faculty's inability to unite and find strength collectively. Despite the best efforts of those who've led their faculty unions, finding unity is difficult, and banding together to advance faculty interests remains a frustrating and sometimes futile task. It would seem the fear of negative repercussions leads many if not most of our faculty colleagues into closeted unionism, unwilling to come out unless they can be assured that no administrator might see them and/or associate them with the perceived evils of unionism.

It's understandable that untenured faculty might be afraid. It's less understandable that tenured faculty live in fear. However irrational such fear may be, it does speak volumes about the culture of an environment in which even many protected by both tenure and their union remain terrified of their administration and what the administration might do to them. Perhaps that should simply speak for itself. It certainly speaks to a need for unionism.

If you are reading this on a college campus, you can look out a window and see a place that has changed in so many ways as to not entirely remain recognizable in the way it was when many of us began this journey many years ago. The academic buildings still remain pretty much the same, whereas the student service buildings, the dorms, and the recreational facilities now often begin to resemble the accommodations one might find in a four-star resort.

Constancy amid radical change. Sanity amid complete insanity. A series of contradictions. If you've survived even a few years of academia, then it's probable that you will have experienced many of the very same experiences as most of us.

Whether or not you bring expertise to the job, there is expertise that is required. The union president will find himself or herself cleaning up a variety of messes made in equal parts by the administration in overreaching attempts to rein in a faculty they often view as out of control and faculty members themselves who sometimes do indeed act as if they are indeed fully out of control.

Some of these messes will require a level of cleaning that no amount of academic bleach, or ammonia, or soap of any kind could even touch. As any custodian worth his or her salt can no doubt testify, sometimes cleaning up a mess means doing the best one can despite the fact that evidence of the mess will still remain.

Similarly, no amount of cleaning can erase some of the marks left by both sides in the stories told. The lack of common sense, decency, integrity, and even humanity that is often displayed by faculty and administration alike is illustrated through a variety of incidents that may strike you as either unbelievable (if you haven't lived it) or as totally believable (if you've lived it).

The personalities may be slightly different, the stories slightly altered, but this is a book that may provide you with the occasional laugh, the frequent head nod, and maybe even a rare rush to anger, or in some cases, a sad and perhaps personally painful episode of wistfulness or even remorse. Some of you may even be called to action on your own campus or within your own workplace based on some of the things you've read and will read here. If such a potential occurrence were to actually happen, those of us who've served our faculties thank you. We know you don't need to do this, and that in itself should be enough to gain the thanks of your colleagues. It probably won't be enough, but it should be.

LESSONS LEARNED

This lesson is simple: you must do everything in your power to prevent your faculty from becoming divided and feasting on itself. Obviously, that is easier said than done, but somehow it must be both said and done. You must do all you can to protect the tenure track. It is the future of the university and the brightest future for *your* university. Your administration may be predisposed to view it differently; you must fight with all you have to impress upon them and all who will hear you that tenure is vital to the future of the university. It is vital to academic freedom, it is vital to attracting the best people, it is vital to morale, it is vital to what higher education is all about. Don't let your administration be the administration that presides over the death of tenure at your institution or even the beginning of the end.

REFERENCE

Sutton, R. I. (2007). *The No Asshole Rule: Building a Civilized Workplace and Surviving One That Isn't.* New York: Warner Business Books.

Chapter Four

Forget about Getting to Yes, How about Getting to Sanity

This chapter begins a more serious discussion of the true despair that can often accompany a person's time as union president. Dark thoughts and paranoia, some of which can be entirely founded, are not uncommon among union leaders, particularly when faculty and administration colleagues make their displeasure with individual decisions or strategies known.

Arguing and defending faculty turf has a tendency to make a person rather disagreeable. Faculty unions are on the defensive. Many citizens, state legislators, and even many fellow faculty members no longer trust or believe in the concept of unionization as they once did.

Don't be surprised if others find you inadequate, uncivil, and at times, even unfit. For those of you who, like many professors, live by an open-door policy, it can become difficult to retain your sanity in the face of a bevy of visitors with a variety of problems and complaints. Recognizing the reality that your time in this position will simply be different and will require different campus experiences is something better known before the fact. Some of those experiences will almost surely cause you to close that door, at least for a while.

Slowly and tentatively at first, out of fear of what might be said, the door will begin to inch open again, if only a bit. Eventually the door will swing open again, and life should return to a sense of normalcy on campus that you might never thought would return. Things may never be "normal" again, but a sense of normalcy may have to be close enough.

Although the tone and tenor of this work may at times seem to border on the dark and desperate times faculty members face in the wake of the many absurdities that surround us, all in all, this isn't meant to suggest that the life of your average faculty member is all that difficult, at least in relative terms.

Life on a college campus isn't coal mining or deep-sea fishing, for though it's undoubtedly more dangerous than it's ever been, it still isn't all that dangerous. It can be mentally dangerous though, particularly for those of us who still try by going beyond our "normal" responsibilities of teaching, research, and service in an effort to make the campus a better place for our colleagues and ourselves. The key to that last sentence, perhaps, is the phrase "for those of us who still try."

Many faculty members have been emotionally abused for so long by so many above them administratively that, frankly, they no longer try. It's a tremendous amount of talent that could be better utilized if the administration only had the good sense to instill in people even a slight sense that the administration valued their work and their humanity. But, alas, that doesn't appear to be happening anytime soon.

The value of the work done by faculty unions may be one of those things we take for granted, and as such, it may truly be missed only when unions are eliminated altogether. Although that day may not come soon, it may not come soon enough for many administrators and political leaders. Many of those leaders envision a future without the collective action of the workers getting in the way of unfettered administrative decision making.

Perhaps those decisions will be made in the best interests of the institution and for the betterment of all involved, but it's hard to imagine that life without unions will improve working conditions for the workers. In fact, if unions weren't good for workers, then it's unlikely that employers wouldn't be so dead set against them all the time. On university campuses, the evaluation of whether unions are good for workers or whether they are antiquated relics of a bygone era is really up to those who are there and who see the realities and consequences of negotiated terms.

Who does an evaluation obviously will affect how an evaluation comes out. We can see that reality play itself out in the world of politics to the world of friendship. Something that a friend says always carries more weight than that which is said by a mere acquaintance. Criticism, constructive and otherwise, isn't always received in the same way it was intended to be received. Praise, constructive and otherwise, isn't always received in the same way in which it was intended to be received.

We are now visitors in a realm in which many of us don't even share the same "facts" with other people. Not sharing facts wasn't something most of us in academia ever saw happening, but it does suggest that much of what seems surreal that surrounds us on a given day is no longer outside the realm of possibility. Whether social media or politics or both are to blame, it is a new reality for most of us.

Perhaps, then, the only evaluation that really matters in the end is one's own evaluation of self. Did you do the best you could do? Did you give the effort required? If the answer to both of those questions is yes, then that should be enough. If the answer to either is no, then you've failed your own self-evaluation. With that in mind, this chapter considers how a person appropriately evaluates his or her time as president of a faculty union.

The question proposed in this chapter boils down to whether time as a union president tends to be an exercise in leadership or merely an exercise in futility. Clearly, it depends on who is doing the evaluation. The larger question may be whether union activism in higher education more generally is a worthwhile pursuit or merely an exercise in futility and a possible method of immolation. In essence, these were the worst of times, and the slightly less than worst of times, and the pages to follow will hopefully allow the reader to evaluate whether these times bear little or no relationship to their own academic or nonacademic situations and collective and individual crises, or if in fact the resemblance is uncanny . . . and, more to the point, unsettling.

So there it is; an objective (truly, what a concept) evaluation of a person's stint as president of the faculty union may differ depending on the standards one uses. Any semblance of objectivity that one might find in evaluating any other person, let alone a union president, is probably lost on every college campus where each union president, however selected or elected, comes from within the faculty. That necessarily means that each union president carries some baggage into the job.

A union president will be able to find colleagues on campus who feel they may be the best union president ever, just as others could be found who may have labeled them the worst. Anyone considering this position or who knows anyone considering this position would probably find others evaluating your or their presidency similarly.

All of us who take these positions exhibit leadership that probably lies somewhere between ongoing brilliance and abject incompetence. The case can likely be made that on certain days, each of those extremes can be matched.

> Teaching is understood as intellectual work; that it is, indeed 'work' in the richest, most generative sense of the word; that it can be improved through inquiry and investigation; and that it's a fit and proper subject for exchange with colleagues who just might be interested themselves. (Hutchings et al., 2011, p. 112)

> Teaching is, after all, a form of show business. (Martin, 2007, p. 86)

When most of us get into the "business of teaching," we genuinely have no idea nor aspiration to actually get into the "business of teaching." Most of us just want to teach. It seems like a decent way to make a living, and most of us actually enjoy the work we do while we contribute (if only in some small way, and if only in our own minds) to the greater societal good. The business side of things often comes later and taints, in a very significant way, our views of the teaching profession and even our views of self. Most of us never, even for a moment, believe that we will join the ranks of the beleaguered until we do.

In the case of a faculty union leader, the beginning of the end tends to arrive once you assume the responsibility of faculty union president presiding over a faculty union. This almost inevitably sad ending is particularly true if you serve as your faculty's lead negotiator for an upcoming faculty contract. For many of us, it is all too clear that we brought all of it upon ourselves.

Most leaders (of any organization) have at least some innate belief that they can "do it at least as well, if not better than those who have done it before." Some of us have been vocal critics of past negotiations or the more general past performances of our former or current leaders.

For many, it always seemed as if the administration had gotten the better of us during contract negotiations and that our faculty negotiating team either wasn't as prepared or as able as they should have been. That perception causes great consternation and a willingness to be outspoken and involved in union doings at a level most of us never consciously imagine until we find ourselves actually involving ourselves.

Criticism may be borne out of equal parts individual hubris, the collective frustration of one's peers, and/or simple naïveté. For the union leader, one's union life begins at conception, the conception of an idea that you need to speak publicly about a union issue.

Although many people tend to say crazy things in public, most union leaders can probably look back at a time when they spoke up at a meeting and they, perhaps even to their own surprise, were heard and seen as reasonable. It's a pretty heady thing to believe that others actually care about your view on things. Clearly, such a belief has a tendency to play upon people's egos and "force" them to be more outspoken than they otherwise would've been.

This isn't the first book to suggest that one's ego can get in the way of what should otherwise be better judgment, and it probably won't be the last. Issues of ego are very real on college campuses, where highly educated people deal all day long with other highly educated people, and proving one's worth in such an environment can lead to many regrets.

That said, most of our peers throughout our universities frequently choose to manage their anger about university slights and wrongdoing by simply ignoring them. Turning the other cheek, as it were, is probably among the healthiest methods of dealing with injustice in the university. Completely ignoring union matters until they affect an individual directly is quite common among faculty members everywhere.

Most faculty members, at most institutions, don't attend union meetings unless and until the end of a contract nears. Many others barely engage in committee work "required" of them by contract. The level of disengagement seems remarkable.

But as with so many conundrums, it is difficult to truly determine whether the disengagement of faculty led to the administration's complete lack of trust and belief in the faculty as a whole, or in contrast, whether the administration's complete lack of trust and belief in the faculty as a whole led to the disengagement of the faculty. Either way, it has happened; it has most surely happened, and those of us present in the moment can feel it all around us. After all, a truly poisonous relationship requires two truly poisonous sides, and in many colleges and universities, both sides fit that description perfectly.

Despite massive growth at many universities, there nevertheless often remains a seemingly uncontrollable need for administrations to extract significant faculty concessions when contract negotiations come around. Perhaps it is as simple as administrators advancing their own self-interests by impressing their trustees with regard to their short-term fiscal management. Whatever it might be, it is becoming more common that at many places, the only thing for certain is that the next contract will be worse than the last one.

Contracts commonly now see the end of step systems for raises, which is always the best means of advancement and was often the sole method allowing younger, untenured faculty members to rise economically to the place occupied by their older peers. Other contracts seek the advent of merit pay to silence critics (of which there are many) and reward boot-licking toadies (of which there are always even more). Higher contributions to health care and lower university contributions to retirement, both during times of rapid university expansion, are now frequent "gets" for university administrations.

None of the administration advances against the union and unionism generally truly should surprise us, at least those of us who have been paying attention. At most universities, trustees are about as corporate and conservative as could possibly be amassed outside a Republican National Convention. They don't come naturally to the concept of valuing unions or unionism as a concept.

The notion that unions should be treated as some sort of partner in a university's advancement also seldom extends beyond absurd and patronizing rhetoric. It must be said, the level of absurd and patronizing rhetoric can at times be pretty impressive. The desire to form a "partnership" with the faculty union for the betterment of the enterprise is frequently a significant theme, and perhaps that partnership could be formed were unions and their leaders more willing to part with raises or even the protections afforded by tenure. Absent that willingness on the part of unions, there can be no meaningful partnership. Secrecy, duplicity, and contempt seemed to describe the union leadership's perception of how many administrators deal with their faculty.

Notifying a membership that an administration doesn't seem to value their collective work presents yet another set of contradictory reactions. Many faculty members already understand and agree with the conclusion that their administration does not always, or even often, have the faculty's best interests in mind when it comes to . . . well . . . almost everything.

Other faculty members, often those least likely to ever attend a union meeting, seem incapable of imagining a world in which administrators aren't simply trying to do the best they can for all of us. Seemingly, the only thing standing in the way of decent administrators everywhere and making their lives unnecessarily difficult were the belligerent union rabble rousers.

Some of those "do-gooders" would proclaim to all within earshot: "If we'd just be nicer, we'd no doubt get as large a raise as the university could afford and as many benefits as they could give us." These words may seem impossible to believe outside of a world of make believe, but nevertheless, that is the world union leaders often face.

Union leaders might find themselves between a rock-hard administration bent on devaluing faculty in every possible way and a faculty whose members are split among those who agree with that assessment and those who blame the union (and particularly the union president) for any and all nastiness between the competing sides.

To suggest that many union members don't seem to understand the nature of the adversarial relationship between unions and management would be a major understatement. Many faculty members seem to genuinely believe, despite progressively more punitive and less favorable contracts over the years and the shrinking tenure track, that simply asking the administration to be nice to us would get the job done. Perhaps that is the nature of academia, where truth is supposed to carry the day. If we "deserved" more, we'd get more, and if the university were truly in financial crisis, then we'd have to understand that we'd have to get less.

This reality is, unfortunately, reality most everywhere on college campuses. Perhaps it's just not in the nature of faculty members to believe the worst about those who seemingly share their search for the truth. One of the most difficult things a person might face who takes on the role of union leader is to somehow disavow your constituents of the notion that the administration is anything other than an adversary during collective bargaining negotiations. We all wish it weren't the case, but it's the case; so we need to acknowledge it and attempt to provide a united front in a war in which the faculty seems always to be on the defensive.

Imagine, hypothetically of course, that a first offer to a faculty union is for zero percent raises over all four years of the proposed contract, combined with cuts to retirement, increases to health-care contributions, higher course loads, changes to the bargaining unit that would lessen the influence of tenure-track faculty, and other generally demeaning language meant to exert greater control over the faculty. Seriously. Imagine it.

Now, imagine some of your colleagues on the faculty, albeit a minority, thinking that the only appropriate union reaction should (or could) be "Thank you so much for doing all you can for the university. Where do we sign?" It is mind boggling in its absurdity. It is mind numbing in its painful reality.

Many a university's "academic capitalism" parallels that broadly spoken of by Thomas Frank in the magazine *The Baffler*, among other sources. It is becoming all too common for universities to rationalize and outsource countless aspects of their operations in a search for cash and for a university to fight its workers nearly as ferociously as a nineteenth-century railroad baron. Frank suggested the reason for some campus authoritarianism stems from the fact that the administration is looting the academic enterprise.

Whether or not Frank is right and administrations should be viewed with that level of extreme jaundice, it seems undeniable that university presidents are unlikely to make a genuine effort to interact with faculty and improve the climate on a unionized campus. There simply hasn't been a lot of evidence to the contrary, nor any real need for university administrators to make an effort to improve the lot of university faculty.

Particularly in light of the success in recent years that administrators and some state legislators have had in diminishing the influence of unions generally, and those involved in higher education particularly. After all, the public doesn't necessarily sympathize or relate to highly educated people who "have their summers off." The perception of college faculty from those outside the walls of academia doesn't tend to lean toward concern for how hard they work or how difficult their jobs may be. In fact, public perception tends to run quite to the contrary, which doesn't improve the leverage of a university faculty when conflict inevitably arises between what an administration thinks is good enough for its faculty and what the faculty would prefer.

Although the president of your university probably makes an outlandish salary, the real culprit is more likely the proliferation of university administrators more generally. Benjamin Ginsberg points out that in the past thirty years, across higher education generally, the administrator-to-student ratio has increased while the instructor-to-student ratio has stagnated.

In the past ten years, administrative salaries have steadily risen while custodians and groundskeepers suffer the inevitable budget cuts—as do students, whose tuition and fees supplement this largess. "In this era of neoliberal graft, universities barely pretend to care about the ideals upon which higher education was founded" (Salaita, 2015). Some of us have been railing about the injustices we perceived were happening on our campuses for years. Sometimes we lament injustice rather quietly, and sometimes less so.

Naturally, of course, there were other expenditures beyond the proliferation of administrative positions that contributed to the disconnect between traditional academia and the corporate academia of which we were a part. Administrators and trustees who had to approve vast expenditures appeared to value student services, lavish buildings, and other amenities (as long as they weren't faculty offices or classrooms) far beyond any value that may have been placed on anything academic.

Tilly (2008) wrote that when things go right or wrong, people have a fundamental need to assign credit or blame so that someone should bear the privilege of having caused the success or wear the burden of having failed. "They don't settle for attributing the consequences to luck or fate" (p. 4).

All of us discuss, both formally and informally, who deserves credit and who deserves blame. Credit and blame, after all, allow us to assess justice in the way that makes us all feel comfortable . . . or at least as comfortable as we can feel as we assess justice. It is a burden placed upon all of us as we are forced to judge one another and assess justice by suggesting and recommending that promotions be awarded or denied and that tenure be granted or withheld.

The multi-talented comedian/actor/author Steve Martin wrote: "Perseverance is a great substitute for talent." In the case of many college professors, and certainly in the case of the one writing these words, perseverance has pretty much been the secret to success. How many times did we want to give up on writing those dissertations that led to our doctorates? How many times did we think, whether because of departmental politics, or lack of initiative, or any number of other things, that we would never actually finish the damned thing? But in the end, we finished our dissertations and got our degrees, which led to our professorships. Usually, that achievement was less the result of talent and more the result of perseverance.

Keeping our dreams rather limited and realistic and our dissertations focused on the achievable rather than reaching for the stars may lead to limited success, but at the same time, it's led to a minimization of failures. "Realistic dreams" don't make for huge success, but at the same time, of course, realistic dreams also require relatively little risk.

This realistic dreaming provides another cautionary tale for those in union leadership positions or for those considering union leadership positions. Our union's initial counter to the administration's proposal for the new contract was pretty standard stuff: we asked for far more than we knew we could get in an effort to arrive somewhere in the middle when all would be said and done. Pretty standard negotiating stuff. No dreaming, no idealism, just standard "we'll start unrealistically high, they'll start unrealistically low, and we'll meet somewhere in the middle."

Predictably, when presented with our initial counteroffer, the administration expressed outrage and horror. It was as if we truly wanted to shutter the doors of the place with our outrageous and unrealistic demands. Did we really mean to cause people to lose their jobs? How could the administration possibly work with us when we weren't even facing the realities that higher education is up against? However seriously overheated their immediate rhetoric might have been, it won the day . . . and the first day was an important one.

Even looking back, it's difficult to know whether we did the right thing. Certainly, we didn't want to start too low because anchoring would no doubt take effect and we'd probably end up meeting in the middle between low and lower rather than the more traditional ending position of somewhere between high and low.

Still, it's difficult not to wonder whether taking the high road and suggesting a realistic, less negotiable "reasonable" place to land could've short-circuited a lot of nastiness along the way, ultimately resulting in more favorable terms and a more lasting peace, but there's really no way to know. For those facing the initial offer and trying to conjure up an appropriate counter, it might be interesting to try the second approach, but obviously, thinking about things in the abstract is far easier than dealing with the reality of contract negotiations.

Had we truly anchored ourselves to a low number, it's very possible that things would've gone even more poorly than they did. And yet, it's difficult not to second-guess, for maybe we truly could have opened an entirely new chapter in administration–faculty relations rather than merely perpetuating the same old same old.

Understanding the bargaining term "anchoring" when it comes to negotiations is a critical place to start for a union leader in considering both the administration's positions and the union's positions. You should assume that the other side understands it, and they probably do. Making sure that the other side understands that you understand anchoring is important. Sometimes, you may need to appear far more prepared than you really are; mostly, though, you will actually need to be prepared, and understanding bargaining strategy clearly doesn't come naturally to all people. So if it doesn't come naturally to you, your level of preparation time just increased.

Faculty members' service to their university and the larger community cannot be separated from their experiences with their administration. A president of a union suffers from those experiences, almost without exception. The experience changes a person's on-campus reputation among his or her peers as (usually) being someone of integrity and a solid work ethic and generally good character, to being someone lesser than many had hoped. It's difficult to imagine a scenario in which accepting this type of position can improve one's standing among one's peers.

The truth is, we are living ever more in an anti-union environment, and "winning" in a contract negotiation against a university administration is becoming more difficult than it ever was. The odds are very much against a union president achieving gains; instead, it's far more likely that a successful union president will merely be able to stem the tide flowing against collective benefits.

Stemming a tide isn't likely to be considered a success. It would be nice if the union could go on the offense and put the administration on defense, but that's a Herculean task and given the larger environment, it may simply be impossible.

Negotiating against highly compensated administrators assigned to that task and against legal counsel employed and compensated to achieve a favorable contract for the administration can be a humbling experience. Despite the confidence you may place in your own and your team's abilities, you go to war with people who aren't teaching full-time and who sometimes, it seems, hold little regard for the profession of teaching generally. Many administrators clearly hold little regard for the profession of teaching, which colors the tenor of negotiations from the onset.

Perhaps many professors reading this might reflect upon times during their own careers when an administrator offered up a colleague's syllabus or otherwise appeared to suggest that teaching a course isn't really all that complicated. Order a book, write a syllabus (or steal one), and go to work. The insult of that aside, the reality of that mindset is similar to the mindset of many who quickly thank military veterans for their service and laud them as the heroes that they are while they wouldn't wish that lifestyle upon anyone they loved.

We admire those who serve our country, but apparently not enough to pay them particularly lucratively or to seek that career choice for our children. Although all generalizations are inherently flawed—and of course there are many people who choose a career in the military over any other viable career—in general, most people with means choose for others to be the heroes and for themselves to sit back and watch.

Similarly, many administrators "admire" those of us who teach, but not enough to really value or even truly investigate what it is that we actually do. The disconnect that exists between administrators and trustees—particularly those who have never taught—and faculty members is significant, and it doesn't help us reach a "meeting of the minds."

But although the administration/faculty disconnect is one thing, the larger issue for those of you contemplating union involvement involves faculty/faculty disconnect. Union involvement is thankless, time consuming, and subject to the criticism of colleagues, who tend not to be privy to what is happening and what information is being shared among the parties to the negotiations.

Faculty members who are protected the most tend to be much more silent than those who feel wronged, who tend understandably to be somewhat louder. Such a reality reflects the larger society, of course, for how often have any of us contacted customer service to compliment someone or something? In truth, we are much more likely to contact customer service to complain. Similarly, a union leader simply must accept that his or her service is likely to result in far more criticism than praise.

In fact, service to your union may change your entire trajectory on your campus, from someone who may enjoy positive relationships with all of those "in power" to just the opposite, and in some cases, it may truly sour decent relationships. It may make "discomfort" the single most appropriate description when it comes to assessing one's presence around certain administrators, and it would probably fairly describe their comparable feelings around you.

You will almost definitely see the world of your university very differently than do many of those around you who hold superior positions. You may be hopeful that such difference speaks to a level of diversity that is appropriate for thinking people at a thinking place, and you may be right, but you may also drive yourself crazy working and functioning in such a discomforting place.

Agreeing to become union president is the opposite approach one might take if one is interested in career advancement, but it nevertheless may seem like the right thing to do at the time. Teddy Roosevelt once said, "It is hard to fail, but it is worse never to have tried to succeed." By that measure (and only that measure), the tenure of many union presidents should be viewed by those of us on the outside of those jobs as an unmitigated success.

If the adversarial nature of the relationship between union president and administration is evidence of that "trying," then the evidence suggests that most of us did our best and tried very hard. We know this if only for the many administrators who have relatively negative impressions of union leaders that they didn't necessarily have before.

If union leaders and administrators still "liked" each other, then perhaps that was evidence that one or both of the sides didn't fight as vigorously as they might have. The politics present in the university and the perils associated with those politics certainly compare "favorably" with the other lines of work in which most of you have engaged in your lifetimes.

The politics of university life is too broad a topic for a chapter in a book. Books about how to gain tenure have been written and read. Part of "getting ahead" in any line of work is necessarily about being liked. If your coworkers like you and those above you like you, your chances of advancement in any line of work are greatly enhanced.

Academic life isn't different in that sense, but being admired is difficult in a place like a university, where many jealousies, some of which may be shockingly petty, work their way into day-to-day matters. The academy is like that; it has been said that we fight so often and so hard because our fights matter so little. Whatever the case, academia remains a tough nut to crack.

Part of what it means to be a college professor is to continually justify one's existence to others. We are constantly evaluated, if mostly informally, by our students in our classrooms, by our administrators who oversee us, and by our peers who offer their takes on our contributions to the enterprise as well as their takes on our personalities, limitations, and general fitness for our respective positions. More formally, we are subjected to post-tenure reviews. As a former union president, having been judged on negotiating skills and the success of representing peers, it almost seems anti-climactic to go back to the relative normalcy of a post-tenure review.

In many ways, a post-tenure review shares a few similarities with an obituary, with the only real exception being the detail of its being written about someone still among the living. The living and the dead, that's the only real difference as we recount the subject's accomplishments, his or her worth, and all of it written in past tense. Of course, there remain hopes and dreams and promises of future accomplishments, but all of that is far less certain than what has already been done, some of which has long been done. Wheelan (2012) suggested that "obituaries are just like biographies, only shorter. They remind us that interesting, successful people rarely lead order-ly, linear lives" (p. 67).

Service to the faculty as president of the union, for better and mostly for worse, further shapes people's perception of the reality of their university and, of course, shapes the larger perception of their own scholarship and their own "place" at the university. Whether serving as a faculty union leader indicates a level of success is open to debate, but what is clear is that such a person definitely will not lead an orderly, linear life.

Union presidents find themselves, at least for a period of time, running almost parallel to the tracks occupied by their peers at the university. You can see your colleagues, and you can hear your colleagues, but you are on a different route entirely, and your arrival at the station is far less certain than those running beside you.

Things one hears, attitudes one feels, all may be damaging to morale and to previously unchallenged beliefs that "you were all in this together." But on the bright side, we educated types truly are in place to "challenge everything" and "question authority" when we believe those challenges and questions need to be raised. Perhaps it's because we've heard so much.

The position of leadership in a union will almost certainly be eye-opening in so many ways. Part of that learning will come by way of better recognizing the various factions within your very own union. Younger faculty may have a sense of intellectual superiority over older faculty, who have a far more impressive sense of irony than the younger faculty. Beyond those two gener-alizations, you may find individuals of many stripes, most of whom have legitimate quarrels with both the union and the administration over the years, and most of whom have no chance of seeing their dreams of reconciliation and harmony make any progress.

LESSONS LEARNED

If you ever feel the need to speak up at a union meeting, be prepared for someone at that meeting to expect things of you. Although your intention may simply be to make a point that you believe others need to hear, those hearing it may assume that if you have the confidence to make such a point, especially if it involves criticism of others, then perhaps you should be prepared to "put up or shut up."

Leading a union looks a lot easier than it really is. Perhaps simply prefacing all stated critiques with something like "recognizing how difficult this job is" or "nobody is suggesting that they could do better" would be a prudent move. Truthfully, though, even such a preface may not matter, for if you really do become active at a union meeting, even if that "activity" is merely speaking out, then you have made your own bed and you should be prepared to lie in it and hopefully not die in it.

REFERENCES

Hutchings, P., Huber, M. T., & Ciccone, A. (2011). *Scholarship of Teaching and Learning Reconsidered: Institutional Integration and Impact*. San Francisco, CA: Jossey-Bass Publishers.

Martin, S. (2007). *Born Standing Up*. New York: Scribner.

Salaita, S. (2015, October 5). "Why I Was Fired." *Chronicle of Higher Education*.

Taleb, N. N. (2004). *Fooled by Randomness: The Hidden Role of Chance in Life and in the Markets*. New York: Random House.

Tilly, C. (2008). *Credit and Blame*. Princeton, NJ: Princeton University Press.

Wheelen, C. (2012). *10½ Things No Commencement Speaker Has Ever Said*. New York: W. W. Norton & Co.

Chapter Five

Seriously, What Was She Thinking?

Should you ever come across a book titled *Disrupting the Culture of Silence*, you'll notice inside the front cover the following dedication: "This book is dedicated to those facing and fighting injustice in academia. We stand with you." In your role as a union leader, such a dedication might resonate with you because you will be one of those both facing and fighting injustice in academia.

Most of us who see ourselves as interested in the pursuit of justice don't normally receive acknowledgment for our struggles on campus. So we should probably be happy to receive some credit in those rare cases when credit is given, even if the credit is indirect and not necessarily intended for us, if only because part of the struggle of being union president lies in fighting injustice every day . . . and losing most of the time.

The exhaustion that comes with fighting the good fight and losing most of the time parallels what is often felt by those fighting truly worthwhile battles against seemingly insurmountable odds and historically entrenched systems in which powerful interests have little desire to see change or often to even recognize or acknowledge that any injustice exists. It's one thing to fight and lose, but it carries a certain greater humiliation to fight injustice and have your adversary fail to even acknowledge that any injustice exists.

Fighting injustice may be worthy of *your* time, many administrators often seem to say, while making it unmistakably clear that fights over such "trivial" things, however cute, are definitely not worthy of *their* time. Most administrations have the luxury of not concerning themselves so much with issues of "justice" and can remain focused on wages, hours, and working conditions. Faculty members don't always have that luxury, and because individual faculty members don't, their union leaders won't either.

There is a tremendous amount of humility that is often involved in arguing some of the admittedly "smallish" things that union leaders must argue. Unfortunately, that humility frequently results in a loss of standing and credibility at best and full-scale humiliation at worst.

As with our country's criminal justice system, justice as a noble concept is often outweighed by the reality of differences in resources that each side brings to the dispute. Outside of academia, people face the financial difficulties that occur when they "fight city hall," while inside academia, it's not money that is lost; it's time and political capital. Sometimes David beats Goliath, but usually the side with the greater resources (typically the prosecution in the case of criminal defendants and the administration in the world of higher education) prevails in the end.

In most union encounters with university administrations, you will likely be sorely overmatched as you and your team, with perhaps the help of a lone union representative from your national organization, face off against a team of university attorneys having the defeat of the union (in any given case) as priority number one. In contrast, as full-time faculty members, your devotion to your cause can only be as great as the number of hours you can devote to any individual matter. Unlike the administration and the administration's lawyers, you won't be able to simply devote all of your resources to fighting the other side because you cannot cancel your classes, your student appointments, your research agenda, and whatever else your university requires of you.

When negotiations begin in earnest, if your union allows or requires the union president to lead the negotiating team, you must select a team of trusted colleagues, all of whom will be out of their elements, and all of whom will have teaching, research, and service occupying their time. It is unlikely that you'll be provided a team of lawyers, and there will probably be no administrative or even secretarial support.

It will be, for certain, David versus Goliath, and David may not even have a slingshot. You may very well have justice on your side, but we all recognize what little power, at least in most contexts, that brings with it.

Facing injustice in academia as president of your faculty union is the central tenet of that role and will consume most of your time, most of your leadership days. Fighting that injustice is far more difficult than you might imagine, largely because there is simply so much more injustice than you might imagine.

That said, some of the injustice was not only more than can be imagined; some of it may actually *be* imagined. A union president's ability to react to—and his or her sensitivity to—what might be called "whiffs of craziness" clearly will need to be sharpened. The ability to distinguish between "full on hard core crazy" and "merely a crazy moment" also has to be rather keen.

We are all familiar with the old adage suggesting that everyone's problem is the most important thing to them at that moment, even while it may not register extremely high on our own importance scale. As a union president, this rings profoundly true. "Problems" come forth and are presented with great anxiety, great gnashing of teeth, and sometimes even great passion and anger. Those problems often seem greatly exaggerated from the point of view of dispassionate advocacy.

The union president will also almost certainly be subject and witness to moments of almost unbearable rudeness, incivility, and downright stupidity. These moments are not the exclusive province of either administrators or faculty, because both are quite capable in this regard.

If you can be patient rather than angry, eventually, you'll be laughing, or at least functioning appropriately, rather than agonizing. But "eventually" doesn't come quickly. For every completely incompetent adversary, there were other only slightly less incompetent people who could find numerous ways to ruin a given day and who seemingly had hours to devote to it. Finding oneself in surreal situations is the province of a union leader, it would seem, so accepting that reality is critical in making any decisions to become a union leader.

As one ages through an academic life, it is also evident that many of the truly horrible people eventually disappear. Although it often takes years longer than it should, more often than not, incompetence and/or a lack of ethics tends to lead to a person's downfall. We've all seen it over and over again on our campuses, where administrators rise and then fall. Often, we can see it coming. Often, it would appear that everyone, with the exception of the person in question, sees it coming.

In other words, as a general rule in academia, although justice is often delayed, it is seldom completely denied. The older we get, the more comforting that realization becomes. Because out-of-control egos lead to unchecked "imaginary" power, it seems as though sometimes the best course is simply to wait until the tenuous limb of power upon which many stand faces a storm and snaps off, propelling the person back down into the pit of despair (or back to faculty status, which in some cases is pretty much the same place).

Not everybody who does truly awful things receives justice in the end, but all in all, it seems like most of the people who deserve to go, ultimately go. Of course and unfortunately, they are often replaced with people who are no better and whose egos put them on the very same course, but again, we simply must wait.

The ability to work with disagreeable people is no doubt a function of most workplaces inside or outside academia. Most of us have probably personally found great numbers of people to be utterly disagreeable. This fact alone suggests at least as much about us as it does about them, but still, that doesn't lessen the fact that some people are simply disagreeable. They are unhappy all the time. They find, often by looking for it, unhappiness in places that others would not. Not unhappiness in the clinical depression sort of way, which none of us would ever diminish, but rather unhappiness in the temporal workplace way in which every petty slight and every petty comment becomes magnified many times over.

Faculty colleagues tend to be quick to judge, quick to find fault, and slow to express gratitude. This quick judgment combined with slow gratitude seems prevalent even if and when they may find themselves benefiting from the work done by their faculty colleagues negotiating and working on their behalf.

Unhappy faculty members may be in many ways less difficult to endure than inexplicably happy faculty members. Perhaps this seems counterintuitive, for wouldn't it always be more pleasant to be in the company of an eternal optimist than the infernal pessimist? The answer to that is, at minimum: it all depends, and very possibly, the answer is simply no.

Many "happy" people, particularly happy faculty members who appear blessed and thrilled to have a job that involves indoor work and no heavy lifting seem always willing to accept anything the administration would feed them without complaint, without question, and seemingly without any semblance of wisdom or thought. The Stepford Professors? Pity the students in the classroom dealing with these folks who seem, for lack of a better term, unquestioning. How could a professor be so incurious? How could a professor lack a minimum level of cynicism?

Although these folks may not be a majority on your or any campus, they are very present and very willing to let the campus community know how lucky you are to be in their presence and how happy they are to just be . . . present. Alive. Taking up space.

But what's that got to do with being a union president? Plenty. People who are simply happy to be employed and do not ever question their administration's motives must be understood so that they can be controlled. Although "control" may seem a harsh term, the reality is that if they aren't controlled they can become . . . well . . . out of control.

Being out of control can mean that they might fail to keep their lack of curiosity to themselves. If they have the courtesy to keep their lack of interest or curiosity to themselves, we can all suffer them with gladness, but if they start to share those feelings, they can make the world of a union president a much harder place.

If, for example, they ever take to all-university e-mail or some other public forum to make sure everyone knows how unreasonable their union was being in demanding something from them, the apparently ever-reasonable and ever-friendly administration, your life will be exponentially harder. The administration will know of the discord within the union and will do all they can to exploit it. If the administration is truly able, they will seize upon that knowledge to alter their negotiating positions, knowing that some faculty members will be more receptive than they otherwise would've and should've known.

These interminably happy faculty members seem to have an ability and a willingness to suck up to all above them. Are they actually seeking administrative jobs? Sometimes. Are they actually just too simple to recognize when an administration was taking advantage of them? Almost always. Encouraging them to keep their thoughts to themselves or to express them only to the union rather than to the entire university, including the administration, has the potential to take up far too much of your time.

One of the first things an incoming union president definitely needs to do is to "demand" (as best as one can) that union communications, both positive and negative, be kept private. At a minimum, they should be kept away from administrators because most administrators don't need help in understanding how fractured faculty unions tend to be.

But enough about the difficulties of dealing with the collective, however appallingly frustrating that can be. It is dealing with certain individuals that really takes the time of the union president. Even before one becomes union president, you will almost certainly know that there will be people inside the faculty union who will make your life difficult. No matter how naïve any of us may be as we enter this type of position, we nevertheless are aware that certain faculty members take up the time of the union president far beyond their relative numbers in the grand scheme of things.

In the police world, it is often said that if a small town could get rid of a few families, crime would basically be eliminated. We don't all commit crimes to the same degree, nor do we all create necessary actions on the part of the union officers to the same degree. The squeaky wheel really does get the grease and certainly the lion's share of time and commitment.

Rationing one's time, as union president, must be a constant concern. Union presidents must make sure that their devotion to the larger cause and their perceived definition of the greater good includes not more than the appropriate amount of devotion to all the many smaller causes that seem to pop up day-to-day.

Much of the blame, of course, with how little success unions are often able to achieve and how little power we are able to wrest from the administration in the service of the faculty lies squarely with union leadership. Too often, it seems we are compelled to deal with the little things and the day-to-day micro-aggressions that faculty members face, which leaves precious little time and energy to truly sacrifice time for the larger battles. In some instances, that might be part of an administration strategy all along. It's painful to give them that much credit, but if it is true, it would be an excellent plan on their part.

During one's time as union leader, you almost have to abdicate any notions you might have had about being "nice" in favor of being practical. People will mostly and eventually forgive you, and knowing that going in could be a major advantage in your self-preservation. Wanting to be liked or caring about being liked too much can and will lead to major errors in judgment and some truly unfortunate decisions. Do not, for example, give out your home phone number in an effort to show your constituents how much you care about them, even if you genuinely care about them.

You need to care more about your own well-being and your desire not to be bothered at home by those taking advantage of your goodwill. Don't think you won't be called at home . . . you will be called at home. Whatever advantages there may be in allowing people to vent at all times, those advantages are outweighed in the instances in which you couldn't actually do anything to appease their anger or disappointment.

Even before taking office, you will likely be visited by longtime faculty members who are probably already known to you as active participants in the union and active thorns in the side of the administration. Sometimes, they may want to lay the groundwork for what will come when you actually do assume the union presidency. They may do so by letting you know that the person in the role at the moment isn't living up to their standards but that they have high hopes for you. If it seems like these folks had little hope for your predecessor but far more hope for you, you should be alarmed, indeed you should be alarmed.

Presumably, like a romantic relationship in which one partner begins the relationship by cheating on his or her prior partner, the subsequent partner might be wise to detect a potential pattern. A faculty member who cozies up to the next union leader largely by rhetorically beating down the prior union leader should be expected to treat you the same way someday.

You might find some of these folks rather charming at first because they tend to be thorns in the side of the administration, but that charm dissipates quickly as you come to almost immediately recognize that they will not merely be a thorn in the side of the administration but that they will also be a major thorn in your side. Dealing with the "issues" of these folks can take an inordinate amount of time, and even merely taking their calls and making them understand that they are valued can take far too much energy that could be better reserved and spent later on more "collective" endeavors.

One problem that is insurmountable for a union president is infighting between and among faculty members. The "thorny" folks seem to play an outsized role in much of that infighting. Although we can't always love or even like each other, a union is weakened greatly when we spend valuable time merely trying to avoid having individual members kill one another. Sometimes, the hatred and animosity for a colleague within a department can be all consuming for a faculty union member. The hatred can become so visceral and complete that there is a danger of one or both faculty members becoming completely unhinged.

Being a union president and having to watch one's back at every single thing an administration does is time and mind consuming enough. You cannot be confronted by a dilemma in which a union member wants the union to take action against another union member.

Although both parties may fully apprise you of the incompetence and general malfeasance of the other, you must do your very best to achieve neutrality. Short of suggesting that one of them look for another job so that they won't have to hate going to work each day, there really isn't much to offer. The union can't effectively discipline a member for being disagreeable. We'd all be subject to discipline in that case. Some of us would be completely unemployable.

The union isn't going to seek the removal of professors from tenured positions "merely" because colleagues in their department couldn't stomach being around them. The union isn't about to get involved in a contest between two members. Making each member understand that can be brutally difficult.

It's certainly understandable how much people may want action to be taken against others who make their lives miserable, but such action would be the administration's job, not the union's. Such a concept shouldn't be all that difficult to understand, but depending on how truly bad people's circumstances or perceived circumstances may be, it can be nearly impossible to suggest to them that the union isn't able to fight their battle.

You must do your best to prevent the administration from infringing upon a member's academic freedom and prevent disciplinary actions that are viewed as violations of due process. You must also do your best to reassure each member that the union isn't picking sides but instead simply does what a union does: protect its members from unjust outcomes sought by the administration.

LESSONS LEARNED

Truth and justice, of course, often bear little or no relationship to reality. You, as a faculty union leader, should know, of course, that you will have zero control over administrators, but you must hope that your social capital with your colleagues on the faculty will carry some weight with them, and they might appreciate, if only for your sake, the need to help you keep your promises.

You must also understand that you will almost certainly be going up against an administration side with far more time and resources to fight you than you will have to fight them. Somehow, making your membership aware of the odds against you can only be helpful to you as negotiations and other dilemmas arise along the way. You must attempt to do a first-rate job of impressing upon the membership the need for unity and the value of the collective. Perhaps you might channel your inner Ben Franklin, "If we don't hang together, we will surely hang separately."

Chapter Six

Mind If I Park Here?

Imagine the following scenario: you are sitting at your desk, perhaps preparing for a class or wondering more generally what the day will bring, when a colleague wanders in with an issue that has always been among the most perplexing on many college campuses: parking. Far greater minds than most, and minds belonging to administrators and faculty members alike, have wrestled with parking on campuses far and wide.

Most of these earnest and fair-minded people have come away bruised, battered, and without lasting victory. But all that aside, in wanders your colleague, and now you will have your very own opportunity to deal with this vexing and seemingly insurmountable problem.

As you begin this chapter, given that it comes well into this book, much of the absurdity surrounding the leadership position in which union presidents might find themselves should already be clear to you. To seize upon the phrase so often used in today's political climate, "If you're not already outraged, you're simply not paying attention." But, of course, it's easy for you to be outraged now, and it's easy for you to see the absurdity as you read this after the fact. It's always far easier to engage in Monday morning quarterbacking than it is to recognize how to handle a given situation at a given moment in time.

Handling a situation in the moment is almost always more difficult than it appears to us later, after a period of reflection. All those clever things we would say in the spur of the moment tend to come to us a bit after the moment has passed. Much of the knowledge we wished we had at a given time similarly tends to come later—often too late, sometimes far, far too late to be of any actual use.

We've probably all watched so many movies over the years in which the quick-witted dialogue makes us yearn to be as immediately brilliant and articulate as the actors appeared to be in the moment. But alas, in almost every circumstance in which something immediately brilliant and witty needed to be said, it came to us later, if it ever came to us at all. Having a team of writers behind you to prepare your dialogue for any possible outcome would be terrific, but, unfortunately, it isn't likely to be your situation.

This theme of "lateness to the game" is at the center of this chapter. Prior to assuming the role of union president, you had likely always assumed that issues surrounding parking on college campuses involved the kind of intractable problems that simply couldn't be solved. As such, those wouldn't be the type of problems that would ever come across your desk. Like peace in the Middle East, it seemed like solving parking issues on campus would be something that would be nice to seek but futile to try to actually achieve.

One doesn't have to become president of one's union to understand the parking problem on university campuses: too many cars and not enough parking spots. This is America, and whether we are ever going to be "great again" or not, one thing is for certain: we want to park close to where we are going, and if we can't, there's going to be hell to pay and someone is going to have to pay it.

It will be a morning like most others, when a colleague of yours will stand at the threshold of your office and, as it turns out, very likely at the threshold of your sanity. You may not know him well or at all. Perhaps you will surmise that you've seen him at various meetings and that he taught math, or science, or in some other department with which you only have the slightest familiarity, but beyond that he may very well be mostly a mystery to you.

We all know the various characters at play in the university. Perhaps their ages or faces or even their genders are different for you than they may be for someone else, but we all know them, even when we don't know them personally.

All too often in academia, opinions are formed and become rather entrenched about certain characters within the cast making up the performance that is a college campus, and that is often because we all know or think we know the characters. Some of them are overly self-important, insisting on inclusion upon nearly every committee or as many committees as they can. Others, in contrast, are completely aloof, and if we didn't know better, we'd really think they were adjuncts coming in to teach a class and then leaving as soon as the class was over. Some people were always in good spirits. Others were always on the verge of an angry outburst.

Despite all the differences in demeanors and general personalities, many of the characters shared one common trait: a bitterness about the parking situation on campus. For some of us, the early risers or those with the early classes, parking isn't necessarily a great concern, but for others, those who don't get to campus early and/or those who teach later in the day and into the evening, parking woes sometimes become almost all-consuming. Those of you who teach in the city quite obviously face a different set of parking challenges from those of you who teach on suburban or rural campuses, but almost all of us face some level of parking challenges.

Although parking may not be front and center on your list of concerns, particularly if you practice early morning arrivals and consistent morning class schedules, it nevertheless would be a topic of conversation among some of your faculty colleagues. All of us can at least occasionally understand the concerns directly, particularly on those occasional days of a late arrival necessitated by a doctor's appointment or other life circumstance.

Frankly, there were times when some of us, if our class schedules allowed, wouldn't even bother showing up if it meant a late arrival. Arriving too late meant that the search for a parking space would involve too much hassle, too much frustration, and too much dependency upon the random kindness or schedule of strangers.

It doesn't take being elected to the role of union president to find dependence on random kindnesses to be a rather tenuous approach to life; it probably just takes advancement into middle age to take a bite out of that particular mindset. Having either direct or indirect knowledge about parking difficulties means that it's not as if we couldn't be sympathetic. Most of us know how dismal it can be to be a late arriver. It's just that most of us hadn't moved that particular dismal circumstance to the forefront of our concerns about dismal circumstances.

Maslow's hierarchy of needs in academia likely places the acquisition and maintenance of tenure as a top concern of most union presidencies, along with those pesky wages, hours, and working conditions, which left worry over parking somewhat marginalized. Though, to be fair, parking was certainly one aspect of those working conditions.

Once it becomes clear that your colleague's story is about parking, you know his story cannot possibly end well. He is about to tell you that he has accumulated parking tickets reaching into the four figures and he is outraged at the injustice of it all.

Your initial reaction, as may very well prove to be your initial reaction to many issues you will face, may be one of total wonderment, as in "How could you possibly amass over a thousand dollars of parking tickets and not either change your behavior or speak to the powers that be and address this situation prior to now?" Was the faculty member so steeped in his own privilege that parking issues that others faced simply weren't an issue for him and thus he viewed himself as free to park anywhere . . . almost literally, anywhere? Did rules simply not apply to him?

It won't be that easy. It's not simply that rules don't apply to him; it's far bigger than that. It's larger than rules, for in his mind, it will be a matter of injustice. If he came into work in the afternoon and there were no parking spots close enough for him to consider adequate, he just parked wherever, on the grass, in handicapped spots, apparently anywhere his car came to rest. We should probably all be thankful that he put the transmission in park and he didn't exit the vehicle until it came to a full stop. Clearly, we should all be thankful that nobody got hurt.

There will surely be many times during your union presidency when you will feel as though you'd been run over by a vehicle of some description, but this scenario seems too ridiculous even for a union leader, doesn't it? With all the problems in the world—famine, poverty, climate change, nuclear advancement, terrorism, the fact that you can't talk about politics with even close relatives—have we really come to the place in our lives where we would need to spend our education and experiences to fully and ably "represent" the views of a serial parking violator? Could this be your lasting legacy toward the advancement of "justice"? The answer, of course, is that it in fact could be. If you let it be.

So many times in life and in the movies, we see the circumstances of relationships gone bad. "It's not you; it's me," we might hear, or in the right instance, we might even say such a thing ourselves. In a case like the one presented above, you desperately must say, "This is totally you; you are beyond repair, you need serious help, you need serious self-discipline, you may need serious discipline as levied by others. You, my friend, have issues, and I will not be dragged kicking and screaming into this particular foxhole."

This cannot truly be the responsibility of a committed union leader. Perhaps it's best if you hear the above quote merely in your brain rather than saying it aloud, but either way, whether it's spoken or unspoken, it will undoubtedly be in your brain.

Surely, the president of the union is not actually perceived by his members as being responsible for fixing individual parking problems. Could the membership really think the union president's time was so unimportant that he could devote energy to this? (Naturally, you will come to discover that in fact many of your colleagues do believe that the union president's time is uniquely theirs and that the union president truly does have nothing better to do than deal with every slight, no matter how slight.)

You must run from this situation, for it will almost surely diminish you as well as your standing among administrators should you be fortunate to have some standing among administrators. Given the fact that you were elected by your peers as their union leader, you must surely have some level of standing. You cannot really be spending your valuable time away from your professorship duties dealing with this level of absurdity, because not only will it take your attention away from where it needs to be, but it will also mean the expenditure of social and political capital with your administration that you will need to have in reserve for later.

Further, would dealing with matters as trivial as this even further diminish not only yourself but also your union in the eyes of an already hostile and disbelieving administration? By taking up the cause of someone so clearly irresponsible, you most definitely run that risk.

We all fully understand the nature of unionism and the need to protect the members—all the members—but seriously, isn't there some line that cannot be crossed? Isn't there some level of individual irresponsibility for which only the individual being so utterly irresponsible must bear the brunt of any extraction from the situation himself or herself? It will greatly assist you if you are somehow able to impress upon your administration your own reasonableness. Fighting every single battle to the death, no matter how insignificant, is no way to impress others that some things are indeed more important than other things.

For all of the indignities you will ultimately suffer, dealing with parking issues should not be among them. Do your best to find a faculty member, perhaps one who is interested in participating in basically every aspect of campus life (they are out there), and appoint him or her to act as your "parking czar." Problem solved. "Keep me out of it, do what you need to do, do not, under any circumstances, tell me where the bodies are buried," you should instruct your newly appointed czar.

Whatever happens with parking, be determined to stay above that particular fray and not get muddied by the day-to-day parking complaints that were most surely going to come your way. A simple decision to abdicate your power and delegate authority may ultimately go down as your finest hour. Simple delegation of authority, every now and then, should be your modus operandi far more often than you might imagine it should be at the outset.

As time passes, it will almost inevitably become clear that parking issues at your university will, like parking issues at most universities, withstand all efforts to improve them and continue on into perpetuity . . . apparently like the debt amassed by the gentleman I've referred to above. Perpetual parking problems are the province of almost every university, and if anyone can truly solve them, there will be statues. More often, there will be blood. But this time, this one time, don't let it be your blood.

Unfortunately, as it turns out, you won't be able to delegate all authority—a reality that will immediately become crystal clear when your university presents you with its first contract proposal. Your initial reaction to your administration's first proposal may be some combination of horror, contempt, and fear. You must do your best to suppress any verbalization of that first reaction.

In a nutshell, your university's first position is "merely" its first position. No matter how reprehensible and unrealistic it may be, it is best to quietly let it all sink in and make no response until you've had time with your negotiating team to let the dust settle a bit. This is true even, and perhaps particularly, if the initial offer would involve pay cuts or job reductions or major increases to contributions to health care, decreases in contributions to retirement, and various incidental indignities, all designed to get more for less and to decrease the faculty's discretion, freedom, and—seemingly, at least—dignity. Essentially, pay cuts for all, more duties for all, and enhanced supervision to boot.

Many times, an administration's initial bargaining stance would make Ebenezer Scrooge proud. Sometimes, were it presented to Mr. Potter from *It's a Wonderful Life*, it's possible that even he may perceive it as unusually cruel. So the proper response is deep breathing, yoga if you're into that sort of thing, and a few hours away. Follow that with a calm and collected (if possible) negotiating team meeting, and you'll be on your way. Where you'll be on your way to will almost surely be open to debate, but you'll be on your way.

Often, in initial offers made by an administration, different and select sections or schools within the larger university will be specifically targeted, perhaps the natural sciences or architecture. Perhaps more often today, less "practical" units, such as philosophy or religion, may feel the brunt of an initial proposal. Usually, the "weak" will be targeted, but not always.

Sometimes, the administration may even go after departments that are perceived as flourishing. In one such case, the administration went after the university's "crown jewels."

Although nobody would confuse that particular university with the more prestigious Ivy League schools or the elite small colleges such as Amherst, Williams, Tufts, Middlebury, Wesleyan, and others scattered throughout New England, the school nevertheless had its academic strengths. These strengths were widely perceived to be in architecture and in the natural sciences. That school also had and continues to have a world-class sailing and polo program as well as food service, which probably speaks for itself, so there is no need to try to explain it.

Architecture was targeted by the administration as the university sought to increase the loads of the faculty by diminishing the status of laboratory and studio instructor hours as counting in the course loads of individual faculty members. The natural sciences were similarly targeted and in the same manner, through the desire to lessen the value of laboratories as counting toward faculty load.

As one might imagine and to nobody's surprise, most of the faculty members in these two schools were outraged and concerned and turned to their union for help in fending off these challenges. Their negotiating team responded by meeting with the faculty, receiving documents from each, suggesting arguments to be marshaled against the proposed changes, and sharing the course loads of similarly situated schools.

When facing distinct challenges being levied against individual departments, it is surely necessary and valuable to seek input from the members of those very departments. Failure to do so would be representative malpractice as well as political suicide; there's really no rational argument to be made against seeking departmental input.

Why would any administration go after its crown jewels? It's possible that the administration really wasn't that interested in changing the loads. Indeed, it's possible that maybe they were even perceptive enough to know that a union would be forced to spend valuable time "winning" these arguments and thus they'd be due for some "wins" themselves when it came to the things they really cared about, like health insurance, retirement benefits, and salaries. Wages, hours, working conditions is a good mantra to repeat over and over if you find yourself leading your union. Don't let yourself get distracted; in the end, it's wages, hours, and working conditions.

If it's truly the case that the administration has "set up" the union by distracting them and requiring them to defend turf that even the administration doesn't really want to take, then give your administration credit for thinking several steps ahead. But more importantly, you've got to understand the difference between "defending turf" and a genuine "win."

When a union wins a debate over course loads or laboratory or studio hours or other "mundane" specifics of a given department, it's very possible that the administration has in fact managed to be a step ahead. While the union fights the trees, the administration can focus on the forest. While the union maintains the status quo with regard to hours, the administration can forge ahead and attack wages and other working conditions. It's truly an uphill struggle, one in which thinking strategically requires thinking ahead and if you find yourself on the defensive, it's very possible you've already lost.

Individual faculty members of respective schools that will be under attack will likely in some cases be grateful to their union representatives for fighting for them and holding the line, but many others in those same departments will probably be completely oblivious that they were under genuine threat and that the union had even been working on their behalf. That, in itself, will be one of the eternal frustrations you may face in terms of the apathy of the faculty.

Quite literally, most of the faculty will have no idea what the union is doing on their behalf, and unless it directly involves them (and sometimes even when it does directly involve them), they simply will not care. So wins will often go largely unnoticed, and the work expended on behalf of the membership will largely be unrecognized. Losses, in contrast, will be noticed. "Losses," in fact—including real losses that don't deserve quotation marks, like concessions on wage, hour, and working condition concepts—will, quite fairly, evoke much consternation, including much public consternation directed largely at the negotiating team.

Administrations that face unionized faculties quite often face other unions on campus as well. The secretaries, the maintenance folks, and some others may also be unionized. A typical administration strategy is to get the very weakest and least powerful union to agree to concessions and then suggest to the remaining unions that "matching" is necessary for the good of the enterprise. It is a very effective strategy.

It is particularly effective in higher education because many faculty members, particularly those in certain disciplines and with a certain predilection for socialism, collectivism, or communitarianism, who already feel somewhat guilty about their "elite" status in society, may feel particularly guilty about their status and their far superior living conditions as compared to their friends on campus who serve their food, mow the grass, and fix whatever goes wrong in their offices.

Many of the hits that a union takes occur when the administration insists upon matching contracts with regard to retirement or health benefits or some such major outlay. It may very well be possible that the only way to prevent an administration from holding the line in that regard is with the threat of a strike. Unfortunately, the feedback that many union presidents receive from their membership when the "s" word is broached is often one of sheer panic and indignation.

Feedback often indicates that any strike would not necessarily be supported by enough of a consensus to make it effective. In fact, most of the membership, when contacted, may make it clear in no uncertain terms that they simply couldn't go on strike. They will, however, probably make it clear that although they won't go on strike themselves or maybe even participate in informational picketing, they will fully support you and your negotiating committee's right to do so. Go get 'em! We're right behind you . . . from a safe distance and from where the administration won't see us.

It seems that, as with many Americans, despite our relatively high professor salaries (at least as compared to national norms for all vocations), many of us nevertheless basically live check to check and wouldn't be able to come to terms with missing even one paycheck in support of the larger cause. If the loss or delay of a paycheck is too much to stomach for many, the thought of participating in unseemly union activities or of jeopardizing their individual futures in some way is too much for many more.

Such powerlessness on the part of the union is no doubt known to most administrations and most certainly emboldens their stances. Sometimes, that means that although the administration will negotiate most things and even concede some of their own positions, they will hold firm to the notion of some of the union matches.

Without a match, you may be informed by your administration (particularly if they are clever) there would be no agreement, regardless of any of the other aspects of the contract. It becomes strike or concede in an era and environment in which there is almost no possibility of a strike.

The union's ability to engage in rhetorical warfare in such a situation is made more difficult by what becomes the need to argue that faculty members "deserve" to be treated more favorably than other unions on campus. Although for a variety of market reasons that may very well be true, it is nevertheless a difficult public stance to take. The administration will know that if they are capable.

Perhaps the largest of all elephants in any negotiating room centers upon the place of tenure and the tenure track going forward. "As long as it has been possible to pay full-time non-tenure-track faculty and adjuncts significantly lower wages, administrators and tenured faculty have been able to maintain high levels of denial about what this system entails and how it works. Because pay for contingent faculty has taken up so little of the budget, they managed to tell themselves that they don't really rely *that much* on contingent faculty, even as the majority of courses . . . are taught by faculty off the tenure track" (Berube & Ruth, 2015, p. 131). Lessening the number of faculty on the tenure track has become a central tenet of many administrations' unstated, but clearly visible, road maps to the future.

Eliminating tenure is difficult because the concept is usually defended by even those who often hate the practice. So, conceptually, tenure is safe. In reality, chipping away at it happens when those who retire or leave for other reasons tend not to be replaced by a tenure-track appointment. The death of tenure through attrition becomes the plan, and nobody from the administration has to really say it aloud.

"We want to make it very clear that we are not suggesting that contingent faculty members themselves are unprofessional. That is not the problem. The problem is that they are not treated as professionals—from the moment they are hired, to positions in which they lack access to offices, phones, email, libraries, and even parking, to the moment they are given summary notice that their services will not be required next term" (Berube & Ruth, 2015, p. 131).

Union presidents are now faced with the serious dilemma of fighting the use of more contingent faculty while managing to avoid insulting present contingent faculty. It's a difficult minefield to navigate.

At many universities, it has been made clear that the administration wants to create a new level of faculty—full-time non-tenure-track multi-year appointments—a new breed of faculty member with far less status than full-time tenure-track faculty but somewhat more than adjuncts. Perhaps they might be considered highly paid adjuncts or horribly paid full-timers.

Vigorous opposition to the creation of this new tier sometimes forces a given administration to abandon the concept during one negotiation period only to bring it up again at the next. There are always fish to fry for the administration in fighting a union, which allows them to float "radical" ideas and then abandon them, knowing that they will simply bring them up the next time.

There is every indication that wherever your university is in this march toward contingent faculty, it is the future that the administration sees. It is likely that their pursuit of the creation of this new form of faculty member will not stay on the back burner much longer. What's another tier, after all? Chances are that your university already has full-time tenure and tenure track and poorly treated adjuncts, so why not slip in another tier somewhere in between those two existent tiers?

A new tier might be created in which faculty can have slightly more job security than adjuncts, perhaps two-, three-, or four-year contracts, but vastly less pay than tenure-track faculty. For the administration, it kills two birds with one stone: lowering pay for the faculty on average while maintaining the level of "full-time" instructors when the increasing dependence upon adjuncts seems somewhat unseemly to the outside world, including accrediting agencies.

It would seem that worrying about individual faculty members' parking issues wouldn't have been so diminishing after all, for in the end, we have the administration to take care of the diminishing. Between the efforts to diminish on the part of the administration and the diminishing grip on reality that so many of my faculty colleagues seemed to possess, being a union leader can truly be a diminishing experience.

Parking problems, in retrospect, could possibly be your salvation should you throw all of your efforts in that direction. Alas, what should be your finest hour of delegation and understanding of the genuine seriousness and scope of your duties may in the end only serve to deepen your sense of futility and anger.

Tending to parking issues or fixing a few parking tickets here and there might give you a sense of accomplishment, however small, and may even provide a few select individuals with positive feelings about the work their union and their union president did. It's a choice. It's not necessarily a good one, but it's a choice. And looking back, it's not a purely insane one, as so many others you face may seem to be.

LESSONS LEARNED

Some of the lessons learned in this chapter may very well be contradictory. On the one hand, there is value to be had in delegating responsibilities throughout an organization. Not only does it encourage and require the involvement of colleagues; it also frees the leader of the organization to focus on those things that really matter. In the case of a union, those things that really matter tend to center upon wages, hours, and working conditions.

Anything outside of those things, though almost everything might fall under the umbrella of "working conditions," is best left to others.

Delegation leads to proper focus and perhaps makes certain that any level of respect that those negotiating against you might have is reserved instead of being spent upon trivial things that matter very little in the end. Fighting every issue like it is the only issue won't allow for genuine emphasis, rhetorically and realistically, upon the major issues that really do matter. Parking is an intractable issue; it won't soon be solved, and taking care of the parking tickets of the membership not only demeans the role of union president but also may require the expenditure of social and political capital in places it simply doesn't need to be spent.

On the other completely contradictory hand, one should not underestimate the value of small victories. As any mayor worth his or her salt would surely tell you, it's a lot easier to put up a stop sign at the corner of North and Main than it is to solve much larger and more intractable issues that may take months or years to address. If the stop sign makes the people who live around there happy, don't put it off; put it up, and then you've won support and built political capital that may sustain you later.

Perhaps it is possible that fixing a parking ticket or several might build political capital that would come in handy later with your membership, but it may come at the price of spending that capital with the administration. It's also a matter of time, commitment, and personality. Perhaps you really can't see yourself giving your own time or your interactive time with the administration to that particular subject. But depending on the nature of your relationship with your administration and your relationship with your own faculty, it may be worth your time to consider and actually sweat the small stuff.

In truth, the lesson here is that it genuinely all depends. It depends on you, your relationship with the administration, the need to impress upon your membership that you are working on their behalf, and the amount of political and social capital you possess. Some might believe—most probably *will* believe—upon entering union leadership that they'll be sweating far too much of the big stuff and dodging too many bullets along the way to get into the weeds about the small stuff.

REFERENCE

Berube, M. & Ruth, J. (2015). *The Humanities, Higher Education, and Academic Freedom: Three Necessary Arguments*. New York: Palgrave Macmillan.

Chapter Seven

Get the Brooms, It's Time to Sweep Something under the Rug Again

Most university administrations have continually increased the importance placed upon marketing, often at the expense of academic integrity. The importance of this chapter at this place in this book is to let you know that many of the absurd policies and initiatives that may be happening in your workplace are not actually disconnected from the union presidency.

Even those things that seem utterly apart from the union may and probably should be viewed as a window into the minds of the administrators you'll be going up against at contract time. And fair is fair. For administrators reading this, the reaction by faculty members to issues of academic integrity that seem apart from wages, hours, and working conditions will likewise tell you much about where a faculty stands.

Does an administration really care all that much about academic integrity? Does a faculty really care all that much about academic integrity? Knowing where each side stands will prove to be important because it's a near certainty that both sides will cite integrity issues during contract negotiations.

The faculty will decry what seems to be the administration's lack of interest in things like improving faculty morale and decreasing workload, which would seem to relate positively to the students' best interests. The administration will decry what seems to be the faculty's lack of interest in things like potential tuition increases, which the administration will desperately want to tie to any improvement in faculty benefits.

We've done some truly phenomenal things in our universities, and many of them have been harmful to our reputations. Many of the most harmful things seem to be done when marketing trumps the academic side of things. As competition for students continues to grow, colleges that can't flourish on their reputations alone find themselves spending more time and money attempting to market themselves in a way that will attract greater pools of potential students. The more who apply, the lower the acceptance rate, the better we'll appear to be, and so on. Rinse. Repeat.

Marketing certain programs is easy; marketing others can be more difficult. Lawyers used to say, "If the facts are on your side, argue the facts; if they are not, argue the law," or something like that. The point is, if your college doesn't speak for itself, you may have to find creative ways of speaking for it. Our marketing department was no exception in their ongoing methods intended to increase the pool and ultimately increase the popularity of certain programs, and your marketing department almost certainly shares many similar traits.

Some of the most remarkable creations that clearly illustrate the creativity of your marketing department and that department's "disconnect" are those that play out in your own academic departments. It's important to know that they will eventually play out in the negotiating room. One such initiative on a university campus involved a relatively short-lived and ill-fated "eight-week graduate course"—a program that seemed to scream loudly that the speed of achieving one's degree was vastly more important than any quality control measures that might be placed upon the achievement of that degree.

One of the most frustrating aspects of the initiative, perhaps the single most frustrating aspect of the initiative, was that there was no faculty discussion or input sought prior to its implementation. The marketing department and/or the provost asked the dean to implement the program. So just like that . . . the program was in place, it was marketed to students, students enrolled, and it was up and running before it was even considered by the faculty.

The legacy of the damage surrounding those sorts of programs tends to remain long after the fact, and the lasting effects of implementation without representation lingers. Although this program itself in all of its ill-conceived glory ably illustrates what happens when marketing overtakes practicality and long-term vision, it also clearly illustrates the frustration involved when those who might offer the best and most relevant input ("the troops on the ground," to use that already overused and often tortured analogy) are not consulted.

There are many aspects of a program like this that are confounding, but perhaps most troubling is the extent to which administrators (some of whom may previously have presented the appearance of being committed to some level of academic integrity) may go out of their way to defend what may seem to be an indefensible program. The soldiers doing their duty, it would appear. The hierarchy demanding that those below support those above. Nevertheless, however rational it might seem, it was still unsettling to see otherwise good people do potentially despicable things all in the name of supporting the corporate bottom line.

Isn't there a breaking point, a point beyond which good people will not allow their rhetoric, if not their actions, to go? We can all appreciate that people need to be self-protective. Jobs are not always easy to get, and families depend on stability and the income that is necessary to provide that stability. Still, can't somebody speak truth to power? Can't somebody just insist on doing the right thing?

Throughout one's tenure as union president, one of the most frustrating things may be the complete disconnect between what your university administration portrays to the outside world and what they portray to faculty. Although the "partnership" between administration and faculty will often be mentioned by administrators when it serves their purposes rhetorically, there is never even a semblance of a genuine partnership in which both parties to the partnership would be treated with respect and given relevant information that affected the partnership and that would otherwise match even the loosest definition of what a partnership would or should mean.

Withholding information from faculty becomes part of the usual course of doing business on many college campuses. Over time, those of us who had been involved in union business came to expect that the administration would always hide anything from faculty that they thought faculty might disapprove of or that might require elaboration or discussion.

Essentially, administrations often adopt a style of "acting now and apologizing later." Many times, in fact and after the fact, apologies will actually be made. University presidents may apologize for a lack of transparency on a given issue and assure a faculty, collectively and sometimes as individuals, that they will do better next time. The fact that this can become the usual course of things can become kind of laughable, kind of predictable, and over time, it simply can become kind of accepted.

"What else could we do?" The administrators lied, they withheld, they moved forward, and what could we really do about it? We'd complain, but eventually, even that seemed like such an exercise in futility that even the complaints became fewer, in spite of the growing list of things that we really should've complained about.

In politics today, many are concerned that today's tone will become the "new normal" and we'll never get back to a time when respect, even in the face of disagreement, is educated adult behavior. On university and college campuses, the same is true, insofar as those things that probably warrant complaints become so frequent that complaining seems exhausting and ignoring becomes more practical.

Learned helplessness is big and getting bigger on campus. In other words, if your administration simply obfuscates and misleads all the time, eventually people will either give up trying to correct them or simply stop listening altogether. Either way, their agenda moves merrily along, and they simply ignore all the criticism. Although we may not admire it and it may even disgust us on many levels, at the same time, one cannot deny the success of it, particularly those of us who don't necessarily believe in an afterlife to even it all out.

This illustration certainly isn't the first time a new program or curriculum change had been implemented without faculty input, or at least meaningful and real faculty input, nor would it be the last. Still, events like this might serve as a turning point for morale and for a lowering of any genuine or even fake respect for administrators, and generally, it may serve as the beginning of the end of a willingness to really go above and beyond for the program.

Any notion of "we're all in this together" is in danger of giving way to "we're not included in this at all." It can serve as a demarcation between past goodwill and collaboration and a future in which cynicism and doubt plague every potential new development.

In sum, things will never be the same, nor will they be as good. Collegial relationships might remain, but a collective sentiment arises and centers upon how much contempt many begin to have for the administration and how little our opinions were valued rather than upon what we might achieve together.

Integrity is compromised or might be compromised when faculty are not consulted as to whether a given academic initiative might be a good, bad, or mediocre idea. For those reading this, such a statement may seem obvious, yet sometimes—too many times, at too many places—faculty are more or less just told that a new program is happening. Marketing. When marketing drives the curriculum, it is at least worthy of a dramatic pause.

Merely because students enroll in a program is not, without more, evidence that the program is a good one. If our goal is to give out degrees more rapidly and get more students and more revenue, then so be it, but surely, we should stop suggesting that there is any other reason.

What about the long term? If there were no studies done before a given program is implemented, how could there have been a plan for any sort of assessment? Will giving people degrees more quickly result in an enhanced program? An enhanced reputation? How will the undergraduate program be impacted? How will the graduate program be viewed? Do we expect that the pass/fail rate of the comprehensive exams might be affected? Again, how would anyone know if there aren't academic conversations concerning the many possibilities?

Union presidents must have an eye on academic integrity because the future of their universities is very much in play, and with that, the future makeup of the faculty. Universities that begin offering "quick courses" may be perceived as "easy" degree-granting programs, and that perception will diminish all faculty in the university, even those uninvolved in a particular quick-degree program.

LESSONS LEARNED

Never underestimate the value of marketing and economic factors in the decision-making process of university administrators. Appeals made to academic integrity will often, if not always, take a backseat to short-term economic considerations. Depending on the academic quality of your institution and the reputation upon which it depends, of course, these factors will play different roles.

Although most of us haven't negotiated a contract at a truly prestigious institution, there is reason to believe that appeals made to reputational concerns might play better there than at institutions on the academic margins. Universities without great endowments and great academic reputations are more fully dependent on the whims of current economic trends. As such, those universities may be less willing to consider academic integrity, worker morale, and other more intangible factors when considering various appeals to reason. Negotiating with your administration will be difficult enough, but it will be made even more difficult if arguments in favor of academic integrity are removed from your arsenal.

Chapter Eight

Another Day, Another Dollar: Another Night, Another Dullard

"It is through constructive conflict that individuals grow, develop, learn, progress, create and achieve." (Johnson, 2015, p. 208)

Pondering the notion of constructive conflict is appealing to many who work in education-related professions. It seems like such a romantic and idealistic notion of what life should be like on a college campus, and the romance and idealism of that certainly appeals to many of us. It's why many of us left the real world long ago, a world in which nonconstructive conflict seemed so burdensome and so ever present.

If you assume your union presidency, the accompanying experiences will likely disavow you of any notion of the idealistic vision of constructive conflict on a university campus. Idealism tends not to square with the realities of administration versus faculty wars on the college campus, in which nonconstructive conflict rules the day. At least most days.

Perhaps ultimately, the "real world" is just as present on campus as it is in most workplaces. It's not as if others hadn't told us that. "There are politics everywhere," they would say, but alas, we never really believed them. The university was a better and more idealistic place, we thought, and we held firmly to that belief until it was ripped from our clinging arms. Reality bites, as it were, and it bites many of us within the university with a vengeance.

Most days such feelings of futility pass quickly enough, but on some days, the feelings of hopelessness linger. Most of us on the faculty still very much enjoy most of what we do: the classroom teaching, the interactions with students, and most of all the conversations, big and small, that we share with colleagues. But some of what we do has become truly arduous. Even some of the "good stuff" isn't as good as it used to be, and the "bad stuff" seems to always be worse. Union activism doesn't tend to enhance the good stuff, but it does tend to exacerbate the bad stuff.

It's enormously frustrating to sense that an employer doesn't care in the least whether you succeed or fail, or frankly, whether you're present or absent. Professors who go above and beyond and who involve themselves in the life of the university, even if some of that life goes toward union activity, should be valued. Frankly, they should be valued openly and in a way that those who do not involve themselves in the life of the university should be encouraged to think about doing.

Everything known about management and leadership, both academically and experientially, seems lost on those above us in the hierarchy of the university. The morale of employees: irrelevant. The pathway to success: nonexistent. Not only would many of us likely avoid running through a wall for our bosses; we often think of running through a wall to avoid our bosses.

Each new administrative fiat seems even more ill-conceived than the last. Outside consultants are called in to assist with marketing; outside attorneys are called in to assist with negotiating contracts with staff and unionized faculty; outside . . . outside . . . outside. There's nothing left on the inside.

Many truly find ourselves in a place where there is no sense of place. Hollow buildings, hollow policies, hollow existences. Work becomes punching a time clock and can be every bit as soul crushing as the many real-world jobs so many in higher education have either avoided altogether or left behind somewhere along the way to search for meaning in our own small corners of academia.

Some of the most soul-crushing experiences at the university, any university, involve meetings. The very worst of these meetings are those that seem so valueless, and the worst of the worst are those that should be effective but turn out to be a monumental waste of time. Some good ideas get derailed by well-meaning individuals trying to do more than can be done or trying to do less than should be done. Other good ideas get derailed by those who don't seem to be entirely well meaning or seem more self-serving than community serving.

Obviously, meetings can be productive and are a necessary reality of academic life, but they can also be mindless, ill-conceived efforts designed more to waste time than to accomplish necessary things. The distinction between what can actually be done by a given committee and what little can be accomplished by any committee remains a constant tension that makes every minute seem unimportant and reminds us that surely our time could be better spent.

The mere fact that something is self-evident is not nearly enough to prevent beating the notion further into submission through analysis, review of that analysis, and then some sort of feedback loop examining the appropriateness of both the initial analysis and the review. Universities are crawling with people quite willing to talk and explore concepts worth exploring.

The problem arises not in exploring and seeking "truth" wherever it leads; the problem is in the vast amount of time and effort spent seeking answers to far more mundane and far less worthy questions. Sometimes—too often, actually—valuable time is spent pursuing answers to questions nobody really wanted answered or seeking solutions that most know undoubtedly won't be implemented anyway. Occasionally, we even seek solutions to problems that don't actually exist.

There are also countless meetings in which the beating of dead horses is more than merely the result of the meeting but was in fact the entire purpose of calling the meeting in the first place. Sometimes, after those meetings have ended, the parties to those meetings agree to meet some more to pursue the endless beating a bit more at a later time, convenient of course to all. Although many of us in academia are not necessarily proud of rhetorically beating dead horses, it's sort of what we've been conditioned to do.

If you spend enough time working in academia, you'll come to learn over the years that sometimes you and your colleagues might be intentionally placed on committees whose sole purpose is to beat to death certain topics and potential policy decisions that previously formed and subsequently disbanded committees have already beaten thoroughly into submission. Many a young professor genuinely believes that most of that committee work must be absolutely necessary and in the best interests of the collective enterprise. Presumably, it's that belief that keeps them coming back for more. That, and the requirements of the tenure track.

Many committees, unfortunately, seem intentionally designed with the sole purpose of wasting the time of those involved, and usually the participants don't recognize that sole purpose until it's too late. There also seems to be a correlation between the more controversial (or expensive) a certain policy endeavor may be and the likelihood that numerous committees have indeed already been formed to study the direction that the university should take. Paralysis through analysis as an intentional administrative pursuit.

If an issue is studied long enough, there should be a variety of ways to attack the problem, which should, in the end, allow people not to attack the problem at all if that is their goal. After all, there are simply so many alternatives. We see this in the halls of Congress with paralysis when it comes to immigration policy or school safety or a host of other problems that need addressing.

This is particularly true of administrative decision making in the university when the issue involves spending money in the short term to address long-term proposals. All too often, university trustees (almost exclusively businesspeople) believe in the short-term bottom line and how things appear on balance sheets far more than they seem to concern themselves with the future.

Keeping a faculty busy doing things that the administration has little or no intention of actually pursuing through policy is one rather effective way of pretending to share a common direction with faculty. Paralyzing the process by forming committee after committee or by otherwise gumming up the works seems to be an effective way of keeping faculty occupied without concern for what it is they might be accomplishing.

It may be too cynical to suggest that much of the committee work foisted upon faculty is akin to giving prisoners television and magazines to keep them busy, relatively content, and complacent so that any talk of dissension, disruption, or rioting cannot take root. It may be too cynical, but then again, it may not be.

As merely one example of intentional paralysis through analysis, many universities struggle with concepts like improving their institutional commitment to "diversity"—what it means, what it should mean, how it should be addressed, how it actually is addressed, all of it. There have been numerous committees on many campuses that have studied the issue and made recommendations only to discover newly created committees with new memberships formed in the following years to do the same thing again.

Perhaps if the administration received the answer they were seeking from the faculty-led committees, then the committee work could cease, but until that moment is reached, the committee work must go forward endlessly. And so it goes, and so it goes again, and again, and again.

As young professors become older professors, much of that youthful idealism all but disappears. We often come to recognize that what seems like a colossal waste of time may in fact be a colossal waste of time. Although many of us may enjoy wasting time as much as the next guy, we nevertheless prefer for that fruitlessness to be on our own terms.

As many of us age through the process, the truth is that we begin ever more to realize the relative brevity of life and the relative pointlessness of many academic meetings. When one puts these two concepts together, a rather natural conclusion begs itself: life is too short to attend pointless and mindless meetings.

Nevertheless, these meetings do have relevancy to a book about unions in the university setting. Getting to know the "players" on campus and how they are viewed is invaluable when it comes to negotiating a contract. Who is respected and who is not and whose words are taken seriously and whose are not are important things to discover if you can do so.

During one's early days as a college professor, or presumably as a college administrator, one of the best ways to establish the cast of characters at your school is through your participation with them at meetings. We meet our colleagues, our administrators, our deans, our program directors, often some of our non-professor staff colleagues. In short, meetings can be more valuable for learning about who is there than—many times, at least—for what gets done.

Some administrators, particularly at the dean level, can be "lifers." They have been at your university forever, and they aren't going anywhere. Usually, their individual schools seem successful enough, even if they themselves might be pretty reprehensible. Some union presidents get to know individual deans and their reputations for honesty or their reputations for something less than honesty. Some deans become infamous for an ability to tell their faculty one thing and then argue against that faculty to their friends in the administration.

These are not the only two-faced people we will encounter in our years on the planet, but they can be among the best illustrations of it we may encounter, if only because of the sheer audacity of telling one thing to faculty and another to one's bosses above. Many deans get away with it for years, with a faculty actually believing that the dean was supporting them in administration meetings when the dean actually spent as much, or more, time undermining them.

Specifically, during negotiations when an administration may seek program changes to a given school, it often falls to the dean of that school to bridge the gap between what the administration might want and what the faculty might not. Some particularly shrewd (sinister?) deans manage to simultaneously convince their faculties that they are fighting against an administration bent on change, whereas they may be in meetings with the administration promoting it. Magical. Sinister. There's compartmentalizing and then there's real compartmentalizing.

LESSONS LEARNED

Campus involvement is a tricky thing. Similarly, the subsequent visibility that accompanies that involvement can be a double-edged sword. Credibility certainly follows "quality" involvement in campus life. Appearing to care about the community of which one is a part is almost as valuable professionally as actually caring about the community of which one is a part. Those people who can combine the appearance of caring with actually caring are growing increasingly rare. We must appreciate those who are left.

Involvement in your union should be done carefully and thoughtfully. If you happen not to have tenure, then it must be considered even more thoughtfully. Although your courage could not be questioned in such a case, your judgment could be.

All of us involved in academia know many folks who are engaged in the world via social media but for whom actual involvement in the affairs of their local community is limited at best. It is easy to pretend to care without having to do any heavy lifting. It is easier to support union workers around the world via social media than it is to be a visible union activist on campus, thereby potentially alienating administrators who hold much of one's professional life in their hands. Being involved in the union is hard work and comes with personal and professional risk.

Deciding to become engaged in campus life and to become visible on campus is a decision that shouldn't be taken lightly. Once a pariah, always a pariah. Once that label is attached, it is difficult to overcome. Speaking out or speaking truth to power means that those in power will do all in their power to dismiss your views.

Weigh the value of full engagement carefully, and how you measure the value of that engagement may be more of a personal choice than a professional one; just be aware that such a personal choice will definitely affect professional outcomes. Feeling better about oneself is great, and it's difficult to counsel against the notion of doing the right thing; however, if doing the right thing comes at the expense of your professional outcomes and your advancement within the organization, be certain of where you stand, and be certain of how able you might be to withstand any potential outcome.

Unemployed or underemployed but principled is probably not an ideal way to spend one's life. Achieving tenure, obviously, makes doing the right thing much more palatable. Biding one's time until power relationships equalize (at least a bit) is probably the pragmatic thing to do . . . no matter what the right thing to do might be.

Finally, life is too short to spend excessive time in pointless meetings. While active in your union, however, meetings can be a gateway to a lot of valuable information. Disengagement from meetings should probably come after your union involvement, not during. Disengagement from the campus community more generally will almost inevitably occur, to some degree at least, after your union involvement, not during. During your union activist phase, the more involvement, the better, for it is virtually impossible to be overexposed while in this role. Exhaustion will follow, most surely, but if you're in it, you've got to be in it all the way.

REFERENCE

Johnson, D. W. (2015). *Constructive Controversy: Theory, Research, Practice*. Cambridge, UK: Cambridge University Press.

Chapter Nine

"Bootlicking 101"

In fairness to most union presidents, you probably never considered your-selves suck-ups (though in fairness, what suck-up really does) to any admin-istration. Still, most of you probably did enjoy, sometimes in the far, far distant past, an excellent relationship with many of those above you in the academic pecking order.

You may have thought it was just because you were relatively nice and reasonable people, doing relatively nice and reasonable work. "Do unto oth-ers" and all of that. That attitude and even those times in your professional lives, many years past, were probably the best of your professional times.

There were times when you and those above you in the pecking order experienced mutual respect for one another, and those were better times. After you might suffer under several years of mutual animosity and disre-spect, it can nearly be said with certainty that the former is far more enjoy-able than the latter.

But alas, the times have changed, and sucking up seems so far away, and seeing others do it seems so truly nauseating that most of you can scarcely believe you may have been guilty of doing so yourselves years before. Clear-ly, whether this is pure rationalization or not, there is a fundamental differ-ence between sucking up to those who may deserve it (respect) and sucking up to those who so blatantly do not. One can be forgiven, even understood. The other is simply ridiculous and casts those doing the bootlicking in the most unfavorable of all lights.

Many of the same people who seem ever beholden and to consistently bootlick those above them are often more than willing to criticize those below them. In fact, criticism of those below is particularly acute when combined with sucking up to those above.

In the case of a union leader, it may very well seem that many of those who suggest you should perhaps be more deferential to the administration were themselves extremely deferential to the administration. In that sense, they can't be faulted for their consistency because they always put their individual interests at the heart of any issue, and sucking up to those above them had seemed to work for them.

Too much time is spent before, during, and after one's tenure as union president having heart-to-heart meetings with individual faculty members about things that never should have wasted the president's or their own time. So many individuals understand so little about the nature of negotiations that it seems as if some of the old stereotypes so prevalent about detached and out-of-touch professors held far more than a kernel of truth. Hadn't these people ever bought a car? A house? Had they negotiated with their children? Their neighbors? Their consciences?

With many of your colleagues, it may seem as though there will not even be a rudimentary understanding of negotiating or any understanding of adversarial relationships. It will be among your greatest frustrations. Perhaps it is the nature of "high-minded" academia in which being confrontational is just too unseemly. In an adversarial relationship, it is difficult to simply be pleasant and agreeable all the time.

Too many times, when hardened positions are declared, some of your own union members will side with the administration. It's as if the administration is being reasonable and you are being unfair, as if a union bargaining position is your bottom line, in a way that seemingly is too difficult to understand. One-on-one meetings may require you to explain to people with advanced degrees that when they publicly side with the administration during negotiations, they decrease any leverage your already weak union might have.

"And if a group is so unintelligent that it will flounder without the right expert, it's not clear why the group would be intelligent enough to recognize an expert when it found him" (Surowiecki, 2004, p. 35). Maybe many of our peers don't see us as the right expert to lead the group, but how would these people possibly know? Their detachment from the interests of their peers and of the union more generally and their tenuous relationship with reality seem to disqualify many of them from really knowing an expert or even a competent negotiator when they might see one.

There are so many wonderful people in the world . . . truly, there are. Unfortunately, as those of you know who've read to this point, this clearly isn't a book about those people. There are of course good people who show up now and then throughout these pages, but mostly this is a book in which the good people are vastly outnumbered and sometimes outgunned by those with less pure motives, less real ability, and simply . . . less.

Too many really bad people have influenced too many really bad things to suggest that a focus on the negative is anything other than a focus upon a large portion of reality. If only this were a happy story, where all the characters were good and decent and achieved greatness in the end. Unfortunately, that will not likely be your professional experience.

It is not as if you will not interact with good people along the way and before, during, and after your service in the role of union leader, for you most definitely will. Still, when you serve in the role of union leader, the stories that last, that really and truly seem to last, tend to disproportionately involve people who've left lasting unfavorable impressions.

You be the judge of whether many of the folks written about deserve public derision. Try to remain mindful of the difference between constructive criticism and destructive attacks, and understand more fully Johnson's (2015) notion of "constructive controversy." That said, most of the controversy that you are likely to see on your university campus will likely not result in much, if any, enhanced creativity and innovation or high-quality decision making. Instead, most of our controversies have resulted in the opposite: diminished morale leading to less interest in creativity and innovation and decisions made only to address each crisis or marketing opportunity rather than long-term strategic decisions made to enhance the viability of the enterprise.

There will be a lot of that insanity around you. In fairness, given the lofty degrees that most college professors hold, it's probably true that on every campus there is an abundance of self-assuredness that doesn't necessarily correlate to one's collective and individual worthiness. We have, after all, "earned" our credentials, whether or not we continue to earn our exalted status over the course of our professional careers.

Apparently, most of us are quite proud of ourselves. That pride might stand directly in the way of accepting one's role as a follower and supporter of those who lead them in the union.

What makes people who aren't particularly impressive think that they are? Were their parents a bit too into the positive reinforcement thing? Have they been repeatedly rewarded for their inanity and never fully held accountable for their stupidity? Those people are like many of our colleagues, the ones who always know they were and are right, which is annoying enough. But it seems downright unforgiveable in those who not only aren't often correct but often espouse positions that border on the idiotic.

Many of these people simply didn't have enough to do, or at least that is the way it seemed. They had been "phoning in" their teaching for years, and their "research" deserved those quotation marks more than you can imagine. Some simply had to find ways to make people miserable around them. Others dreamed of someday finding a place in management where they could torment entire groups of people at the same time, like so many of our present administrators seem both to do and enjoy.

All too often one runs into faculty members and administrators who seem to think they've been granted special dispensation to be completely self-absorbed. Despite many of our humble backgrounds as faculty members at all kinds of places, we seem to have constant contact with colleagues who seem to believe that they are somehow below their deserved station in life, no matter where they are and how they got there. "This isn't Harvard," we might often hear ourselves saying in meetings and under our breath to those who seem to believe their wisdom as a faculty member transcends common decency.

Perhaps if they were truly distinguished people working at a truly distinguished place, then we'd cut them some slack, but for the love of God, they work with *us*, at *this* place, and frankly, that isn't always a lot to brag about. If you're actually reading this at Harvard or somewhere you consider on an equal footing, then if you find yourself in this type of situation, it may seem somewhat more understandable. It won't, however, be much less frustrating.

Too many faculty members seem to believe that the place they are at is lucky to have them, when in reality too many of them are damned lucky to be in the place that will have them. Their "lifer" status is not always a result of comfort and tenure, and in fact it may actually represent reality and work ethic. Many of us have probably been tempted so often to suggest to some of these folks that they really should be at a better place and it would serve us all if they'd try a little harder to get there.

But alas, the reality for most of us is that we are where we belong, and seeking greener pastures would put us against some stiff competition that would find most of us wanting. Even if some could make it out alive, most would be best served by putting their heads down and forging ahead in their present positions. So why, we continually ask, don't they realize what we realize? Why don't they see what we see? Why should they possess such superior attitudes when there is simply no reason to hold them? Why do people patronize those below them when there really isn't anyone below them? It remains a constant source of bewilderment.

Patronizing those below is often exemplified most clearly when an individual is plucked from the teaching ranks and accepts an administrative position. Although many of us are immediately suspect of someone who would agree to such a thing, we often can distinguish between those who were pressured into it (totally acceptable) and those who bootlicked their way up to it (hideously unacceptable).

Sutton (2007) wrote about them in his book *The No Asshole Rule: Building a Civilized Workplace and Surviving One That Isn't*. It was astounding, he found, how rapidly even tiny and trivial power advantages could change the way people thought and acted. Although you should read the book, you don't really need that passage because you've almost certainly lived that passage.

You will see total transformations of certain individuals on your campus from those who were "good union folks" fighting the good fight against the administration into those who were able to flip their viewpoints immediately upon attaining an administrative position. Things that the administration had said and done to faculty, which were formerly outrageous, suddenly became completely understandable in the eyes of these folks.

Having an ability to shift one's core principles overnight seems remarkable, and yet it became just another example of those who put themselves fully ahead of all others in the quest to find power. It seemed that no matter how little power they actually possessed, they lorded whatever they had over others with a vengeance.

You can try for years to understand how people could change on a dime like that, but reading Sutton's book might help you understand it in the simplest of terms: it's entirely possible that they were (and are) simply assholes. If a person is an ass, then almost all of his or her behavior can be understood and makes far more sense. It would be more confounding for sure if good people acted this way, so there is at least some comfort in knowing.

Too many times during your presidency, you will be confronted by people just about equally divided between those who are well meaning and those who are mean-spirited, who suggest that you pursue things that you would have to be a complete idiot not to have pursued already.

"Why not suggest to the other side that administrative bloat is an issue? Have you suggested that past raises haven't kept pace with inflation? How about bringing up the fact that administrative salaries have risen faster than faculty salaries?" All excellent ideas, you might find yourself saying, as you assure those making the suggestions that indeed they've been issues raised and litigated time and time again. "Maybe if you could just be more respectful." "Maybe you could be more strident and less respectful." Thank you, everyone; thank you so much for your words of support and your unique ideas.

There will most certainly be times when you will believe you've found yourself in the land of Oz or at least some of your colleagues have placed you there. If you only had a brain, or some courage, or even a heart, surely, you could navigate the yellow brick road of negotiations and get everyone the raises they all so richly deserve.

If many of your critics only had the time you apparently had, they all could've done a better job, and they will often seem comfortable in telling you so. Many of your colleagues may tell you, in a true act of shamelessness, that they were simply too busy to take on the mantle of union president, so it was good that you had the time to devote yourself to it. Any irony, of course, lost on all of them, who it would seem normally might realize that you all had the same jobs!

So ultimately, in the most timeless of all condescending notions, you may be thanked vociferously for all the time you devoted to the cause just as you will be condemned (usually not to your face) for the horrible job you had done. After your time as union leader has passed, the new president will face many of the same indignities, and the underlying message remains: "Thank you for all you are doing; if only you could do it better."

LESSONS LEARNED

In the simplest terms, you really need to be cut out for this type of duty. If you are the type of person who wants to be liked or at least may be bothered by the negative perceptions of others, this may not be the right position for you. There's no shame in declining something that you're not really qualified to do. We'd all be better off if people understood their limitations and did the best they could at roles most appropriate for them. The truth is, we all have certain limitations.

If you might be filled with resentment and anger about things that are likely to be said behind your back and/or about the general lack of support from so many for whom you will be killing yourself trying to represent to the best of your ability, this position simply is not for you. Perhaps you don't need constant affirmation, but you certainly don't need constant criticism and continual patronizing either.

A colleague in my own department once stood at the threshold of my office door and proclaimed that he'd offer himself up as union president, but he "was too busy." It's best if you can answer that in terms that don't require impossible anatomical acts and suggestions of what he might do to himself. "Too busy!" We were all too busy!

A suggestion to those of you taking on this duty: know thyself. If you are thick-skinned and somewhat immune to the criticism (fair and otherwise) of others, you are union president material. If you are not, and things—all kinds of things—really bother you, then run for the exit; don't take this job.

You know how some people say that if they had to do things over again, they wouldn't change a thing? As you read this, it should make you ponder the potential wisdom involved in turning down this position should it come your way. If you've truly pondered it and you still feel as though it's right for you, then it might be. May God be with you and/or have mercy upon your soul. Assuming, of course, that your willingness to take this position doesn't directly illustrate a complete lack of any soul. In which case, you may be perfect for this position!

REFERENCES

Johnson, D. W. (2015). *Constructive Controversy: Theory, Research, and Practice*. Cambridge, UK: Cambridge University Press.

Surowiecki, J. (2004). *The Wisdom of Crowds*. New York: Anchor Books.

Sutton, R. I. (2007). *The No Asshole Rule: Building a Civilized Workplace and Surviving One That Isn't*. New York: Warner Business Books.

Chapter Ten

"Merit at the University: The Unimportance of Being Earnest"

Much of this chapter may require the following disclaimer: if you feel old, increasingly out of touch, and perhaps nearly obsolete, your perceptions of place will necessarily be different than if you remain young, vibrant, and viable in the life of your institution.

There is some value in recognizing your place, but merely recognizing and acknowledging it won't necessarily make you feel better. In fact, if you recognize yourself in this chapter, then this may bother you in a myriad of ways and the reality that your best working days are so clearly behind you may only buttress your belief that you left so much on the table back when you could've done something about it.

But as depressing as all of that is, there are some advantages to finding oneself increasingly invisible, not the least of which is less involvement in futile and time-consuming committee work. Many of you reading this may have the finely tuned perspective honed over the years of someone who was hyper-involved in your university's life. But now you may find yourself transitioning into someone who tries desperately to avoid involvement in what you may know to be exercises in complete futility.

Most of us who have some years at the university under our belts have likely seen our own participation wax and wane then and again. Sometimes, life gets in the way, and other times, the university itself gets in the way. We probably all know of many colleagues over the years who have persisted in their total and complete engagement, and just as many (actually probably far more) who've managed to live their lives almost completely disengaged from university life.

We should all have an even greater and newfound respect for those who involve themselves in university life. Not everyone is cut out for union work (though it can be annoying that more aren't willing to make the sacrifices necessary to work on behalf of their colleagues), but all of us can be "involved" in aspects of university life. Attending university events and supporting students in their organizations is vital to a truly vibrant university.

Total disengagement is impossible and would be inappropriate for any professional in any professional setting, but at the same time, it is increasingly difficult to find oneself fully immersed in the workplace culture when the culture may be so horrifically poisonous. So a decision will someday be upon you, and that decision seems to beg for taking steps to decrease your involvement in campus life, beyond your work with students and attendance at sporting and cultural events. It will be for your own mental health.

One method that many faculty colleagues have used to navigate the diminishing culture is to become more involved in the "virtual" world becoming more prevalent on college campuses. If "orange is the new black" and "fifty is the new forty," then teaching online is the newest form of campus engagement. Like so many surreal aspects of academic culture, teaching online can become engagement without involvement. If this seems like nonsense to you, rest assured it seems absurd to many of us as well.

But the future is now, and although many of us struggle mightily to embrace it, most of our universities have fully embraced it—for all the right reasons, no doubt. Increasing revenue would be one take on why the concept has been embraced so fully and so quickly. "Enhancing the educational experience" would likely be the university's take on why it should be embraced.

At any rate, giving online education a virtual hug and touting its virtues and integrity seems both antithetical to the genuine process of education and the beginning of the end with regard to any real need for any "real" professors on a college campus. The increasing use of online programs has a vast array of implications for unions, ranging from intellectual property rights to the archiving of classes, to the credentialing of faculty involved in "virtual" classes.

In Michael Moore's classic documentary *Roger and Me*, there is a scene in which General Motors assembly-line workers cheer the last vehicle as it leaves the line in a plant in which the workers are to be replaced by robotic arms. Moore suggested that there was a basic incongruity between cheering the advancement of technology and the loss of one's job.

Although the movie is now rather dated, the point remains a good one, and it is one that should resonate with us as we "embrace" to varying degrees, of course, the onslaught of virtual classroom experiences and the accompanying need for fewer of us in the classroom and fewer of us generally. It seems as though we should be reluctant to cheer such a development and reluctant to accept that this particular change is for the better.

Although many of us find ourselves spending hours on our computers doing constructive things like writing and mostly useless things like visiting our Facebook pages every now and then, it still hopefully must strike us that our real lives are better than our virtual lives. Real engagement, real time with friends and family, real activities like playing golf and going to the movies seem to provide far superior memories. For most of us, this is undoubtedly paralleled by our own academic experiences with real professors and real-life interactions. It's unimaginable that someday people will remember their virtual classroom experiences with the fondness and vividness with which the rest of us remember some of our own real experiences.

As a college professor, there is perhaps nothing better than the occasional past student who reaches out in some way (even virtually) to tell you that you had an impact on his or her life. Knowing students only through a computer, even if they can sometimes see us and we can sometimes see them, seems to make these potential impacts "virtually" impossible.

But the previous paragraphs notwithstanding, we must assuredly come to accept that we cannot survive this atmosphere and this culture if we unilaterally disarm. Throughout this work, it's been suggested that we tend to have weak unions in academia and that our collective power is mostly imaginary.

Most academic unions are simply not altogether strong given the widely disparate views and perceptions of their many members. Although recognition of our collective weakness remains true, individually we are even more susceptible to injustice and administrative fiat. Being weak together is incrementally better than being completely weak alone.

Taking an individual stand against virtual educational experiences on a college campus where we could better focus on real educational experiences will only get us so far, and frankly, that isn't very far. So as we peel off any remaining vestiges of academic integrity and cast aside any shred of residual personal dignity and self-respect, we must get on board and find ourselves one by one occasionally teaching an online course.

Even if we think the concept is mostly ridiculous and speaks to the end of quality education as we once knew it, it is nevertheless the future. To deny it is to stand idly by while the powers that be change the locks on your door and move your belongings out to the curb. Wanting to remain moderately viable in such an environment of change, we probably feel compelled to occasionally participate in all that is wrong with education today. It is what it is, as they say.

All of that said, there is most assuredly a place for online education. Students who live far from campus, in rural areas, or who have full-time jobs demanding their time all seem excellent candidates for nontraditional methods of delivery. Most of us, maybe all of us in higher education, are on board with that.

What we may not be on board with are programs that are online to appeal to students who otherwise could very well take traditional classroom experiences but who simply choose not to do so. Can we be certain they aren't cheating? Can we truly be certain they are doing their own work? Most of all, can we truly be certain the value of their programs is fully legitimate?

A dirty little "not-so-secret" in academia is that on search committees, many applicants with degrees from online universities are simply not treated the same way as those with degrees from traditional universities. Perhaps it's unfair bias or tradition gone wrong. Whatever it is, it's very real.

Would you want your own son or daughter to eschew a traditional college and choose an online program instead? Most of you reading this, if you have the resources to make genuine choices, would not choose online for your children, and you know it. We all know it. Whether we take pains to deny it or not, we all know it.

Allowing ourselves not to live in denial of the reality that now is all around us and understanding that the money that flows into university coffers that is so valued by administrators and CFOs makes online classes very real and very much a part of our academic lives is how we now must function. Faculty members have to do what faculty members have to do, and they have to make their own decisions when it comes to teaching online. But the more favored that delivery system becomes with administrations everywhere, the more difficult it becomes to avoid getting on the online train.

Many faculty now teach an online course every now and then to supplement their income (often undeniably necessary in today's administrative environment in which yearly raises are paltry). Many faculty members lost step raises years ago, so their yearly raises, when adjusted for inflation, are now barely able to keep them at the same level from year to year.

Many of our standards of living as college professors were better ten years ago than they are now, and that is what our economic future will continue to be. Given all of that, that a faculty member might find an overload or teach online or otherwise do extra work to get a raise in their pay that they otherwise wouldn't get, seems entirely practical.

Muddling through and seeing the abandonment of meaningful step raises over the years creates a different culture on campus than many who entered higher education ever envisioned. In such a culture, the thought of making more money might become a much more significant consideration for many finding themselves in less viable financial positions than they were counting on when they were initially hired. In such a low-morale environment, not only might online "opportunities" begin to thrive, but it also suggests that the laboratory for "merit pay" on campus is ready for occupancy.

Despite all that is collectively wrong from a union standpoint about an individualized system like merit pay, it nevertheless garners some support even from those who truly should know better. It doesn't take much effort to consider the long-term implications of merit pay upon a union, but self-interest has a way of blinding people to a lot of otherwise obvious long-term implications.

As you read this, try the following experiment: grab your smartphone or your computer and search online for the phrase "merit pay and unionism." One doesn't have to be a seasoned researcher to determine that the concepts don't adhere well to each other. Unions are about collectivity, protection and advancement of the members, and hopefully the betterment of all. Utilitarianism at its finest. Merit pay, in contrast, is about individual advancement.

If contracts really are zero-sum, if we are truly only going to get as much money as we can wrangle out of the administration and no more, then how that money is divided and whether it is for the advancement of all or the greater advancement of some is at the heart of unionism, or at the heart of anti-unionism. Why do corporate leaders seem to love merit pay? Why do increasing numbers of university administrators ever more bent on modeling their workplaces using corporate America as their guide seem to yearn for more merit pay?

In an effort to completely and probably unfairly boil down the debate over merit pay, as many of us have witnessed it, into two camps, consider the following: One camp consists of younger and more arrogant faculty convinced not only of their own brilliance and the conceptual worthiness of merit pay but also their innate superiority that necessitates differentiation from their lesser (usually older) peers; the other camp consists of the more collectively interested faculty, more prone to harken back to genuine union days when solidarity trumped individualism. As if wholly representative of the true problems with many unions, and with an academic union in particular, the question boils down to "Assuming the amount of collective money is the same, would you prefer that all members receive a 2% raise or that some receive 4% and others none?"

Perhaps not surprisingly, for some the answer depended upon whether or not they deemed themselves worthy of a higher raise than their peers. There are some of us who are able to combine our own self-esteem with a higher calling for collectivism, but many have difficulty thinking of the whole before they think of themselves. Of course, in their defense, most faculty at most institutions had already lost step raises from past years and were feeling an economic crunch that many had never anticipated.

Many professors face the payback of significant student loans and are seeing what was once considered a comfortable lifestyle, that of a tenure-track professor, slip away from them. The reality that younger faculty were by and large never going to see the living conditions of some of their older colleagues can be daunting and is another arrow in the quiver of administrations bent on dividing faculty from one another and further weakening already weakened unions.

Perhaps it's far easier for older faculty to believe in more collective action, as to some extent, they've already gotten their piece of the pie. So perhaps it could be argued that each side was equally selfish and self-interested.

That said, it was suggested early on in this book that there would be some blame placed upon certain parties to certain disputes, so while apportioning that blame in the words that follow may not seem entirely fair, it should not be entirely unexpected. As such, from the perspective of a union leader and a true believer, and from the perspective of the one who is writing this, the narrative shaped here essentially pits those who believe in the collective good against a bunch of self-serving narcissists.

One particularly significant divide has become ever more noticeable on many university campuses: the divide between relatively (in most cases) young and sometimes untenured faculty members and their older and tenured colleagues. Although the divide has been forming for years, it has only seemed to grow, and it is reflected, at least to some extent, in the positions many members on both sides of the divide take with regard to merit pay.

A faculty that loses "step," or longevity, raises is a faculty that is in a different place from a faculty that has not. That loss, which has profound implications for the future pay of all but those at the top of the pay scale, is often a significant reason many people become union activists at the level at which they do.

That the old should make more than the young is not in itself unusual or controversial. What happens, however, with the elimination of steps is that it can become clear that newer faculty members would *never* make the kind of money their older peers did. Talk about the reverse side of the American Dream: not only would the younger generation not make more than their older counterparts; they would never come close to making what the older folks made (at least in relative and inflation-adjusted terms).

Any anger that is engendered, though very real and significant, is mostly relegated to self-interested groups (and aren't we all). Many younger faculty tend to be angry about their inability to make more money via "merit." Many older faculty don't much care. Obviously, there are exceptions to this rule, but most of the exceptions involved people who still didn't have the personal need, drive, conviction, ability, or whatever to become genuinely involved in the union. So fully understanding their positions, held privately, is difficult to do with great clarity.

For those who do care, on either side of the issue, sides are taken and battle lines are drawn. Faculties begin to function ever more as divided faculties (something that all administrations everywhere must, no doubt, relish). Dividing an already weak union into two distinct self-interested factions would do the type of lasting damage to the union that administrators could only dare dream about prior to the loss of step raises and the advent of merit pay.

So any union president with the benefit of this insight might do well to see this coming. Resist the elimination of longevity raises with every fiber of your being. Not only because of the anticipated consequences of a lessening of the money paid to faculty, but also because of what you should now recognize as an inevitable divide among your faculty.

Divides among and between certain factions within the faculty may not happen immediately, but they will surely happen. Money is serious business, and even people who don't generally go into the profession of teaching to become rich nevertheless fail to find it amusing when they feel as though they have been disadvantaged in relation to others.

Over the past few years, there is an impression that the divide between young and old has deepened. Although both sides are always to blame in any divide, perhaps those of us who now must self-identify as older faculty members cling to a belief system that puts more responsibility for the divide upon the young. The younger side, through their rhetoric and sniping, has truly been responsible for increasing the depth of the differences between us.

Still, it actually parallels the "trophy culture" that many of our younger faculty portray at our institutions. In sum, some younger faculty members seem quite willing to suggest that they are simply "better" than the rest. They work harder, they are smarter, they care more about the students; they are, in a nutshell, "better." Thus, they deserve more, and as a corollary, older faculty deserve less. Even if that were true, and in some cases it no doubt is, and in many other cases it no doubt isn't, nevertheless it seems extremely discourteous and intemperate to actually say it aloud.

Maybe we now live in a "post-truth" world in which saying what you want to say regardless of its truth or veracity is viewed as part of the entitlement of being a citizen. Expressing one's superiority to others didn't used to be seen as a positive trait, but the world has changed and our experiences inside of academia suggest that the academic world is reflecting that change.

As tenure becomes ever more threatened, as business models trump academic models even inside the academy, establishing your superiority over others becomes more important than any sort of collegiality and/or collective endeavors. It's a dog-eat-dog world out there—and in here.

Merit pay and other "individual" entrepreneurial initiatives seem vital to a younger generation bent on proving their superiority to the older and more traditional members of the faculty. Individualism trumps collectivism again and again. Reconciling that reality with unionism becomes increasingly difficult and makes the union itself seem increasingly irrelevant to many of its own members. "What have you done for me?" not "What have you done for us?" has become the question on the lips of many of our members, and in a hostile negotiating environment, it is impossible for everyone to be a "winner."

So there you have it, in a society in which everyone has to be a winner all the time, negotiating give and take is seen as an unacceptable paradigm. After all, to "take," there must be some "give," and understandably nobody wants to give.

The only successful negotiation would be one in which we increased our pay, decreased our contributions to health care, decreased our course loads, made tenure easier to achieve, and by and large "won" every aspect of a give-and-take negotiation. The fact that such a result is impossible is not relevant to those seeking to get it done. Compromise may now be seen as concession.

Many younger faculty members have time to inform the world, via social media, of the minute-by-minute great and interesting things they are doing and with whom these things are being done. If we're genuinely fortunate, they may even show us pictures of their lunch. Nevertheless, they often will not have the time to attend a faculty meeting to assist in the discussion of the many important things happening in union/administration relations.

There will be time to criticize and dissect after the fact, but there simply isn't time to participate in the discussions beforehand. Perhaps that is the price they pay for doing all of these incredibly meritorious things that make them believers in individual concepts like merit pay. Time is at a premium. Commitment to a cause larger than their own self-advancement isn't frequently in the cards.

One very serious frustration worthy of one's consideration concerns the disconnect between so many of our self-promoting faculty always informing us about how involved they are and committed to "causes" outside of campus, but who would never consider the cause of unionism and collective action and social justice on their very own campus. You know these people; they are quick to support the good citizens of any given country faced with any given level of injustice, but they are nowhere to be found when confronting injustice on their own campus. "If justice isn't everywhere, then it isn't anywhere" could've started with even a minor commitment to their own colleagues, but alas, what would that get them?

There are efforts that a union president can make to improve levels of fairness for the younger faculty in the university's contract (perhaps by accepting higher premiums on health insurance for those making more, in return for lesser premiums for those making less, or through the creation of a parental leave policy allowing a semester's paid leave, or through attempts to make the achievement of tenure less paperwork-intensive). Despite your best intentions, there may nevertheless remain the perception that the younger faculty are not as favored by your union as the older and more established, particularly the tenured.

There is genuine danger down the road in the division between the old and the young and between the union activists and the freeloaders or mostly freeloaders. Someday, if we are not careful, we may all find ourselves in an environment in which putting others first or concentrating on the needs of those most at risk during contract negotiations gives way to the petty infighting discussed earlier in this work. If and when that day fully arrives, it will be the end of unionism in the university setting.

Even if future negotiations actually favor younger people, the prior damage through the elimination of steps may simply be too severe and likely cannot be overcome in one negotiating cycle. Arguably, the damage can never be undone. But again, perceptions are now more comfortably "fact free." It will, of course, be frustrating to hear oneself being portrayed as not caring about the very people who will likely be a constant focus of your concerns. But that is the reality of many "political" figures, and being the president of the union is a highly charged political position—there can be no mistaking that.

Another frustration that is probably shared by far more important people than any given union leader—including, presumably, past presidents of the United States and other world leaders—is that actually changing things in more than trivial and almost imperceptible ways is incredibly difficult, sometimes impossible.

In meetings held about contract negotiations and in meetings in subsequent years about future contract negotiations, many faculty members will come up with grand suggestions about what the negotiating committee should do. These suggestions often occur absent any recognition of what the negotiating committee is actually doing and how hard they may be working to implement those very suggestions.

All of this may strike the reader as the defensive posture of a past and failed president, and that may very well be true. Still, defensive or not, you will find it endlessly frustrating to have people hold so little belief in you and your negotiating team that they seem compelled to "help you out" via condescending suggestions and inferences. Suggestions and inferences that seemed to imply that you simply must not have "tried very hard" to get a better deal for the faculty. Or in the alternative, that you were simply too incompetent to do good work.

Either implication seems rather depressing. But as we all know, perceptions are often more difficult to overcome than reality, and thus, for the most part, at some point one has to give up defending oneself and one's negotiating team and assume the figurative fetal position assigned to all past union presidents, at least for a while.

Perhaps the single most divisive issue facing negotiating teams in the future will be the place of merit pay or something like it in the contract. Administrators and legislators often favor the term "performance-based pay," as if to suggest to all that not everyone who is employed is performing at a high enough level to "deserve" rewards.

Nobody can argue that some are better at their jobs than others. In truth, it's even difficult to argue that all employees are worthy of their paychecks. Every workplace features some individuals who are guilty of less-than-stellar performance. Large workplaces, like most universities, tend to be no different from anywhere else in that regard.

The question becomes, how do we attempt to address strengths and deficiencies in the workplace? And for most of us on the union leadership side, it's long been held that merit pay isn't the means to improve conditions on the ground. In fact, we often argue that merit pay will do more harm than good and make a workplace with limitations even more limited, but that is a tough sell in today's anti-union individualistic environment.

Not all of us are in any way enamored with the concept of merit pay, and those who favor it, as well as those who do not, surely have their own valid reasons. With that as a preface, however, there is some compelling evidence that merit pay not only isn't universally applauded, but that it simply doesn't have a positive effect upon worker productivity. So, put simply, if we don't like it and it doesn't work, why should we want it in a faculty contract? Has there been evidence at the university that merit pay has increased faculty productivity?

Some of us have our own tortured history with merit pay that may be relevant to the context of the larger discussion. After all, we are all indeed shaped by events that make up our lives and our day-to-day experiences. Chances are good that if you don't have your own anecdotes regarding merit pay, you nevertheless know someone who has a good story.

Opposition to merit pay builds over time, brick by brick, one thing after another, the straw that broke the camel's back and all of that. On the campus nearest and dearest to me, it all began a decade or so ago when members of the faculty received a letter from our then president. The letter was in response to faculty union concerns about what to many seemed like arbitrary and capricious decisions regarding the denial of promotion and/or tenure involving certain faculty members.

In response to faculty concerns and in an effort to quell the dissent, the president wrote, "It is my job and that of the Chief Academic Officer to ensure that such decisions are not made in a capricious or arbitrary manner and reflect the thoughtful interpretation of the contract and normative practices in higher education." The quote is verbatim and thus warrants the quotation marks.

It was in that context that a "simple" hiring became a complicated controversy. The controversy began when the president's son was hired. Although, granted, the hiring of one's son over those clearly more qualified is a different circumstance from the president's interest in faculty promotion and tenure, it would seem that the principles of the university would be similar.

If hiring one's son is a "normative practice in higher education," then it is time for faculties to suggest that perhaps a more objectively based system be put in place. One of the concerns many have held regarding the imposition and growth of a merit pay system for faculty has been a belief that rewards at the university have not always been entirely merit based and that merit pay has come to mean "suck-up pay." In fact, there is a belief held by more than a few that promotions and rewards have occasionally been subject to the whims of sometimes capricious and arbitrary decision making based on favor granting, bootlicking, and other nonmeritorious forms of service.

One of our faculty members wrote an all-university e-mail expressing his outrage over such a clearly unjust situation and the message it sent about "merit" on a college campus. One thing led to another, and as one provost was leaving office, she informed the letter writer that the letter had not gone unnoticed by the president. In fact, the university president had told the provost that because of it, there'd no longer be any merit pay for the person who wrote the letter.

In fairness, why should we expect that administrators would be more able than the rest of us to separate personal grievances and slights from professional rewards? Some, no doubt, would be, but others, as this illustration shows, would not be.

Although one anecdote doesn't prove the whole, it's hard to imagine that similar things wouldn't or couldn't happen on campuses everywhere. It would seem that this should be reason enough for not believing that merit pay in the control of administrators on a college campus is such a grand idea.

You could begin resisting the urge to succumb to merit pay as a concept by informing younger faculty and faculty leaders of institutional history. Doing so must be done delicately, because few things are more annoying than older faculty members turning to younger ones and offering to "inform" them about institutional history. It's like gender-neutral "mansplaining."

We must ponder our place in the navigation of that fine line between letting it all go and shouting to the rooftops that the "administrators are coming, the administrators are coming." One if by merit, two if by evaluations, but either way they are coming and they are coming for us.

Still, there's something uniquely appealing to the American spirit about being rewarded for good work. On the college campus, however, it is particularly difficult to always understand what good work is and how it should be rewarded.

Blowing the whistle is difficult. Loyalty to the organization from which we collect our paychecks and derive most of our professional satisfaction is a value that is not to be diminished. Loyalty, however, cannot trump honesty and the values that we hope all of us individually value beyond complicity in the actions of those who hold power over us. If you can be loyal and honest, then so be it; if you cannot be both, you've got to choose honesty because that is the lasting value that will ultimately serve the stakeholders in your organization.

All of us are, after all, replaceable and someday will be replaced. Most of us harbor no illusions that our institutions will continue to flourish after we're gone. Even those above us who may have played a more significant role in the success of our institutions must still recognize that we will not shut the doors after they leave.

The value that an institution places upon honesty as a core value in the learning process must extend beyond any discussions of academic integrity and the oath that, at many universities, students take upon entry into the university. We expect our students to be honest and not use their positions for their own benefits at the expense of justice. We should expect the same standard be applied to faculty, staff, and even our highest-ranking administrators.

Doing something positive and saying something negative when you see those above you do "unjust" things should, we hope, come almost naturally. It doesn't take an extraordinary person to do impressive things, but it does take some small amount of courage to stand up to those who never expect you to muster the strength to challenge their ways.

Many "scholarly types" read so much about segregation and racism and sexism and now "Black Lives Matter" and "Me Too" and "Never Again" and injustice generally that perhaps they are prone to see injustice where others don't. Such insight isn't always right, of course, but it does seem as though many on the faculty are conscious of how those with power sometimes use that power in ways that do not make the world better and in fact lessen all of the participants in a particular community.

Doing things that you can get away with merely because you can get away with them is an exercise of raw power that has no place in a just community. Standing up to those who try is what a just community is all about. Doing so in an environment in which merit pay is on the table is infinitely more difficult. Part of the role of a union leader, like other leaders, should be to pursue policies that make the values of honesty and fairness easier rather than more difficult to achieve.

Whatever accomplishments even an able administrator or faculty member might claim does not grant them immunity from your criticism and your concern when you believe they act in a way that lessens the great trust that is placed in those who hold a powerful position. Sometimes, even good people with honest hearts find themselves in positions where making the right choice is more difficult than making what seems to be an easy choice.

Actions for which no negative repercussions follow tend to be repeated, particularly if the actors are rewarded. Perhaps we should shrug and accept the old adage that it's truly not what you know, but who you know.

Most of us are already cynical when we consider whether a true meritocracy exists outside of the boundaries of our campuses; but don't we have the right, and perhaps even the obligation, as educators to try to strive for a meritocracy on campus? Shouldn't all of us together strive to create a place where there is incentive to do good work rather than simply to suck up and/or stay in the good graces of those who might determine our merit pay?

The danger of inaction is much greater than any present benefits or fears of future retaliation. If anyone is truly afraid of retaliation for speaking truth to power, then we are in a much less powerful position than anyone who uses his or her mind for a living should accept.

Glazer (2002) suggests that an organization counts on the threat of punishment to exercise control over those who might otherwise blow the whistle on wrongdoing that they see. We should stand together and suggest to the administrators who are responsible and/or complicit in all unfair practices that we're more afraid of an institution in which truth and honesty are compromised than we are of any individuals who exercise present power in that institution.

Faculty members have given themselves to their universities, and their universities reflect them as they reflect their universities; it's not fair to ask anyone to look away when they see something wrong before their eyes. Those who would ask anyone to do so should be ashamed of themselves. Those who would respect people for blowing the whistle when wrongs are committed have our eternal respect in return.

In recent years, faculty members at Penn State and Michigan State, among other places, have seen tremendous shame brought upon their institutions by those who use their power and privilege to prey upon others. Any faculty member or administrator who knows of wrongdoing but looks away is not worthy of a place in academia. Our policies should reflect that.

If merit pay were based on merit, then the good would get it and the bad would not. How we defined these terms would be a concern for another time. But we don't live in a meritocracy; educated people even talk about the "myth of meritocracy." People don't always get what they deserve. Some, particularly those on the cynical side, would argue that people actually seldom get what they deserve whether they deserve a lot or a little.

In any case, merit pay is clearly a discretionary tool that can be and often is used by administrators to get people below them to "toe the line," corporate or otherwise. Surely, any thinking faculty member would be able to see that, and when they aren't able to see it, it's the role of the union leader to explain it as clearly as he or she can.

Those in favor of merit pay seem to wonder why those against it would be against "extra money." The flaw in that particular line of reasoning begins with the term "extra," for if the money were available to be doled out based on merit, it would be available to be doled out to everyone. This concept, which should not be difficult to grasp, is nevertheless quite elusive for many people. If there is money available, it is a matter of distribution, not a matter of whether it should be available "only" for merit pay.

Most significantly, if one really does occasionally believe that principles matter more than money, then there is a need to stand firm in the face of the reality that merit pay is clearly used to silence critics of an administration. Faculty members shouldn't be complicit in an environment in which criticizing the administration would put them on the naughty list while only those on the nice list would get extra compensation. It would be only natural that faculty members, especially those who might be younger and those without tenure, would watch their tongues rather than endanger their finances. Academic freedom?

We really shouldn't need more anecdotal stories or more evidence about the lack of merit in merit pay and the desire in corporate America to control employees through it to understand why unions and union leaders would take a stand against it. One need only search online for the term to see how union members generally perceive it or to see how incompatible such a corporate tool is in an academic environment. Still, it was and still remains unnecessarily controversial and hugely misunderstood.

In the end, you can still fight for your integrity, despite what we often know that is worth in corporate America. The suck-ups are still going to suck up, and those with integrity are still going to be treated less favorably than the suck-ups. It isn't going to change, but at least the immediate inequity of greater pay for the favored can be stopped if union leaders stand firm. Standing firm in favor of the collective good can be a small but critical victory meant to slow down the inexorable slide into complete corporatism.

LESSONS LEARNED

This lesson is or should be ridiculously simple. There are certain things for which a union stands: collective action, collective interest, and a general greatest good for the greatest number. Corporate attacks upon unionism should be met with resistance. Attempts to divide members from one another should be met with resistance. Allowing a division to occur transcends any given issue because fissures within a union will eventually destroy any leverage any union might possibly hope to have. A failure to resist measures that so obviously seek to divide the membership would be clear and simple union malpractice. There's really nothing more to say. It's too obvious to require more elaboration.

REFERENCE

Glazer, M. P. (2002). Ten whistleblowers: What they did and how they fared. In M. D. Ermann & R. J. Lundman (eds.), *Corporate and Governmental Deviance* (6th ed., pp. 229–249). New York: Oxford University Press.

Chapter Eleven

Negotiations: Let Them Eat Cake

In agreeing to stand for election for the presidency of a union, you might be required to write a brief synopsis of the reasons for your candidacy in the form of an open letter to the membership. Even if it is not required, it seems like it might be a good thing to do. You might even fill yours with idealism, and hopefully at the time you are writing it, you will actually be filled with that idealism. With the benefit of time, you may come to recognize how misguided (though well-meaning) it all was, but only with the benefit of time.

Having a vision for your organization is vital, even if that vision proves to be somewhat blurred in the end. A faculty association exists, after all, like all unions exist, because of the belief that collective strength was needed to advance the interests of the membership.

If the membership could truly trust the administration to do the right thing, there would really not be a need for a union to protect the members and their interests. The core of any strong university is a strong faculty. As such, a strong and respected faculty union is in the best interest of the entire university community, despite what will probably be administration beliefs to the contrary. In short, the interests of the faculty *are* the interests of the university.

Enhanced credibility as a viable faculty association translates to a greater ability to achieve meaningful involvement in shared governance to address faculty and administrative concerns and positively engage in reasonable negotiations of future contracts. Part of increased credibility means approaching our dealings with the administration as an equal, with the goal of achieving an enhanced level of collegiality and cooperation between the faculty and administration without compromising the strength of the association.

Both the union president and administration's counsel have to answer to higher powers in all matters. Administration counsel has the university president and the very corporate-minded board of trustees breathing down its neck, and the union leader has the membership. Both of those constituencies expect great things from their champions. The job of university counsel may pretty much be on the line, whereas for the union president, the "only" things you really stand to lose are your pride, your reputation with the administration, and your standing among the membership. In other words, what could possibly go wrong?

It's possible that during negotiations with counsel for the other side, you will find yourself sharing some personal common ground. Counsel knows or usually knows that the administration doesn't care about them personally, and similarly, the union leader knows that the administration doesn't care about them personally either. From that common ground, a bit of mutual respect can be gained.

If you do ascend to the presidency of your union, it will probably be for reasons other than the brilliance of your letter to the membership suggesting your worthiness for the position. Do not let it go to your head, because your ascension to the "throne" may have more to do with the desperation of the electorate (another precursor for national elections) or the limited nature of your opponent (yet another precursor for national elections).

It may even have to do with the hard reality that most people don't even care that much about who their union president might be. Among those remaining who do care, you may simply be marginally more popular or may be seen as marginally more capable than your opponent. In whatever means it might happen for you, it may not be the honor you might think it is, and it may not be the time to celebrate your success.

This chapter tries to convey the nature of the negotiating process. The "nitty gritty" of your term as union president will focus, of course, on negotiating a new contract. The team of which I was a part began negotiations earlier than they had ever been begun before. It was our dream to establish a firm groundwork and illustrate to the membership as well as to the other side that we were serious about this and willing to do the hard and long work necessary to get a favorable contract. Why wait until the contract we were working under expired? Past negotiations always got under way only slightly before the end of the previous contract and became serious only very near the deadline. Past negotiations were always contentious.

We saw a different path as a better path forward. It meant that we would have to start devoting many hours to this process early in the spring semester. Asking people to commit to this and keeping everything organized leads to your first very serious decision as union president: the number of people who will serve on the negotiating team, assuming, of course, that your union's by-laws don't mandate who might serve on the negotiating team. If your union by-laws have no such provision, it will fall to the union president to make the selection of who will serve on the team.

If there is no set structure (and there probably won't be), then the team you choose may consist of as many faculty members as you choose. In consultation with the people you trust most, you'll need to make a decision on a number that would provide appropriate faculty representation, allow for a variety of skill sets to come together, and of course, not be too cumbersome. Such a mix is difficult to achieve. On many campuses, it may be impossible to achieve, and yet, that will likely be your task.

Whatever number of team members is chosen, you should look toward a mix of people coming from different academic backgrounds, all with some institutional history—ideally, perhaps even a couple of folks with prior negotiating team experience, all who will assure you that they will be dedicated to working to negotiate the best contract that can be achieved.

As with any group of people, not all will prove to be equally engaged, nor will all be equally committed to working as hard as they might in the end. Regardless, each member will ultimately pay a price with their colleagues. It cannot be said for sure that you will all lose friends, but you will definitely suffer some strained relationships with existing friends and forever damaged reputations among those who will now have a reason to dislike you. After all, a contract is a huge endeavor, and compromises will have to be made.

When a contract agreement is reached, there will inevitably be pushback from some colleagues who won't believe in provisions that wouldn't benefit them directly. There's no way to describe that reality in terms other than as disheartening, and as cementing the perception that eventually unionism in such an individualistic culture may simply shrivel up and die. The idea that college faculty were somehow less selfish than the larger population may die for many of you around that time.

It may very well become absolutely apparent that for many of the "collective members," the only purpose of the union was to make their individual lives better, and if others were hurt, that was of no concern to them. In fairness, most professors probably didn't enter the profession knowing anything about unionism or even suspecting that they'd ever be a member of one. For some of us, though, excusing pure selfishness and individualism as a symptom of a lack of knowledge didn't go nearly far enough to actually excuse it at all.

It can prove to be simply amazing and completely reprehensible how often many of your own constituents may be more than willing to sacrifice others for their own benefit. If the administration wanted to raise the course loads of the architecture faculty, why should the social sciences or the engineering departments care? The notion that you are all in this together will be difficult to convey and will probably be done only with limited success. One for all and all for one can easily become an endangered concept.

Your negotiating team may come to discover that you resemble hundreds of independent contractors far more than you might resemble a group of people with common interests and common philosophies. Naturally, there will be many fine and decent and caring faculty members who truly do view themselves as part of something larger and clearly do put the interests of others above their own. All of you on the negotiating team will necessarily fall into that category (or you better), and many of your older faculty, many of whom may have previously served on past negotiating teams, likely fall into that category too.

If you want to find "true believers" in unionism, you might want to lean toward talking to your older faculty members. Sadly, we all know that unionism as a concept and philosophy and practice has been stronger in the past than it is now. It's simply a truism, no different from perhaps a suggestion that if you wanted to talk about the sport of baseball for any length of time and/or find someone passionately committed to the cause of baseball, your best bet might be to seek out someone over the age of forty.

As with any group of individuals, as time passes and the stress of negotiating a contract heightens, some of the differences among the members of the negotiating team will be heightened as well. Even among friends and trusted colleagues, the stress of the negotiation process can contribute to some pretty nasty individual moments. Through it all, the union president must somehow keep everyone together, at least publicly.

It may be like an uneasy marriage in which, despite your many differences and your growing indifference to one another personally, you nevertheless decide to stay together for the sake of the children. For the sake of the faculty, you must put your best face forward and show what may seem like remarkable unity in front of the membership.

The truth is that you will not always be on the same page as all of the members of your team, nor will they be with each other. There will be days, many days, when you won't be happy with the direction in which you are headed, but through it all, you absolutely must stay together in the most trying of times. Perhaps you might share a copy of this book with your team members. It couldn't hurt. Nor would it hurt the author.

Whether you should select "friends" for your team is a dicey subject. "Know thyself" is perhaps the best advice to be given on that front. Although you may hope your friends will better understand you and would be more likely to stand with you in tough times, negotiating with those to whom you aren't really close is far easier, and any feelings that might get hurt along the way don't linger.

Friends can truly be lost during fierce battles, even when those friends are on the same side, as the tension and frustration builds and sometimes boils over. That said, on this front, there is no correct answer, nor is there even the presumption that any answer might be correct. It all depends. It truly all depends.

In choosing a negotiating team, there is an appropriate place in one's mind for the old adage "Keep your friends close, and your enemies closer." Hopefully, nobody in the position of union president would find themselves picking an "enemy" on the faculty to serve with them, or frankly, even having an "enemy" on the faculty. Nevertheless, it is sound advice to know who among faculty members at your university simply has to be on the team for political reasons. Their absence may do more harm than you can imagine.

Should you choose to make the negotiating group smaller rather than larger, there would be many potential built-in advantages. Meetings would be far easier to schedule, and consensus would be far easier to reach. With a relatively small group, each member could openly muse about potential outcomes without beating dead horses completely into submission. It would also be probable that keeping a unified front would be far easier to achieve . . . at least publicly.

There are merits to a larger group as well because it would allow for more voices and more opinions, but all in all, a smaller number of team members would probably not make your list of regrets. Smaller may very well be better, and larger may very well be less maneuverable in every sense of that word.

What probably shouldn't be done would be to start early or to even attempt to imagine or pretend that your administration would have any real interest in the nature of the academic enterprise beyond bottom-line dollars and cents. Don't waste too much time appealing to academic integrity, the "value" of full-time faculty over adjuncts, and the positivity associated with higher faculty morale upon the greater enterprise. It's noble and true, but it probably won't advance your cause. It's wages, hours, and working conditions, period.

Despite what you might read in the newspaper, despite what your president and the admissions and marketing folks likely say about the brilliant future, the beautiful campus, the new buildings, the increased applications, you will nevertheless be met in negotiations with almost apocalyptic pictures of the death of your university. Higher education is in peril, and institutions like yours are in grave danger. Maybe not today, maybe not tomorrow (and never in your literature or your public face), but soon, and inevitably.

The only way survival can be ensured is to get labor costs under control. Faculty is labor, and in corporatized academia, labor in the university is not very different from labor anywhere else. In other words, labor is simply the cost of doing business, and that cost needs to be lowered.

Although it may seem impossible or at least improbable, success for your administrative team in the eyes of the trustees may be to make sure that your faculty slips down the rankings of pay and benefits for similarly situated schools. The very notion of "similarly situated schools" will likely also be in dispute, as you might imagine the lists of schools compiled by your administration tend to focus on schools that pay faculty relatively poorly. Your list, in contrast, will likely feature schools that tend to have higher pay and benefits. Both sides, as you might imagine, will suggest that the other side's list is patently unfair. In sum, it's highly likely that you won't even agree on your peers.

Trying to come to terms with disparate notions of fairness when negotiating a contract is harder than it might seem on the face of it. Clearly, you won't all agree upon what fairness looks like. In fact, you may not even unanimously agree that fairness should be a part of it. Imagine not agreeing upon the premise before the premise.

As negotiations wear on, it may seem that getting to yes would be every bit as unlikely as getting taller or getting better-looking. You could aspire to it, but in reality, it isn't going to happen. Maybe you'll ultimately have to agree to get to "OK, good enough" and forgo any dreams of actually getting to yes, especially if that means an enthusiastic yes. As time wears on, most of you will settle for settling. Enthusiasm will be long gone. Morale will be low. Frustration will be high.

You may find yourself in a place where both sides are mired in their own "facts." The knowledge, seemingly on both sides, that you can't really both have separate sets of facts may not, without more, prevent you from having them. If you do have them, it tends to make coming to the middle almost impossible. After all, where is the middle between two unrelentingly disparate fact patterns?

The erasure of public memory and the social relevance of education is being forgotten in favor of a language of measurement and quantification. "When we survey the current state of education in the United States, we see that most universities are now dominated by instrumentalist and conservative ideologies, hooked on methods, slavishly wedded to accountability measures, and run by administrators who often lack a broader vision of education as a force for strengthening civic imagination and expanding democratic public life" (Giroux, 2012, p. 117).

It seems as though many administrations not only lack a broader vision; they lack any vision. If your union is in such a place where vision is lacking, it makes meeting the administration somewhere in the middle all the more difficult. Your middle may involve a look into the future of the university, but their middle often reflects only the immediate bottom line.

"Accountability" seemed only to mean bottom-line pricing and measures in the very moment, as if some sort of return to shareholders in the short term was our most important mission. It can be as if the university were truly a business with publicly held shares.

Stanley Fish (2008) suggested a decade ago that colleges and universities should be accountable to "academic values—dedicated and responsible teaching, rigorous and honest research—without which higher education would be little different from the bottom-line enterprise its critics would have it become" (p. 159). Without that level of accountability and devotion to genuine academic values, there can be no real long-term thinking.

Thinking down the road doesn't seem to be compatible with the short-term process of getting a contract that the administration can take to the board of trustees and illustrate their "bottom-line" successes in the moment. You should know that the bottom line will likely be the sole driver of the administrative side, and you should be prepared for it.

That said, it's almost impossible to convey how frustrating it will be to negotiate with people who don't care about what the future will bring as long as they look successful in the moment. Any means at your disposal to try to get people to see the future should be marshaled.

Long-term thinking (strategic thinking, as it tends to be referred to now) can involve money spent now for dividends that occur well on down the road, and given that those dividends may accrue to the benefit of people not presently at the university, there seems to be remarkably little interest in pursuing such lines of inquiry. Running the university as if the university itself and its survival depended solely upon this quarter's balance sheet has become the norm at too many places, and it has largely served to stifle any long-term planning. This bottom-line thinking seems to reflect a common belief that the corporatization of academia continues largely unabated.

"By espousing empirically based standards as a fix for educational problems, advocates of these measures do more than oversimplify complex issues. More crucially, this technocratic agenda also removes the classroom from larger social, political, and economic forces, while offering anti-intellectual and ethically debased technical and punitive solutions to school and classroom problems" (Fish, 2008, pp. 75–76).

Colleges and universities are about a great deal more than measurable utility. They must embrace the long view and nurture long-term critical perspective (Giroux, 2012). If Giroux were in the room with you, it wouldn't be a certainty that he himself could do a better job of advocating for the long-term health of the institution than you could. In the end, it may very well not matter how effective such advocacy might be, because the other side may very well not care. It's difficult to prepare for that going in; hopefully, by reading this, you can prepare for that.

One of the problems that exists at many universities is that the bargaining process has perhaps helped illustrate—or, less grandly, simply served to reinforce—the lack of communication that often exists between deans and the faculty. The reluctance of the faculty to agree to administration proposals centering more authority and decision making among deans is even larger than the obvious "faculty governance" issue at play, which is large enough in itself. There is a basic lack of trust among many faculty and their deans, and much of that mistrust stems from the simple reality that faculty are not included in discussions that would seem to primarily affect their professional work.

Specific examples are numerous at most schools, some of which you may need to discuss with, among others, the university president and the university chief legal counsel. Those discussions probably won't result in anything beyond lip service, but you can't be blamed for trying. It seems as though university administrations often suppress potential conversations with faculty to lessen future potential complaints. What we don't know apparently cannot hurt us.

It's all too common for many of us to lament the fact that basic academic decisions central to the academic enterprise simply aren't discussed. Faculty are "informed" when decisions are made and are seldom included before those decisions have been made.

Even obviously faculty-oriented issues like the direction of a given program or where new hires should be made are not always a source of discussion between and among faculty and administration. Perhaps your university is like many others, and you too will be told that "in the future we'll do a better job of inclusion." But the future comes all the time, and changes simply rarely occur.

Perhaps the most striking example of the complete disconnect between deans and faculty during contract negotiations occurred at our university in the school of architecture. There was a major push by the administration to increase the course loads of the architecture faculty.

Whether increasing the course loads of a faculty would enhance the university's ability to better educate its students and/or increase efficiency and how that would or would not correlate to faculty productivity, morale, incentives, etc. is something that was obviously central to the health of the school of architecture, both in the short and the long term. The fact that only a very few faculty had been made aware of a proposal that would so significantly affect them and that there had been no real or significant discussion between the dean and his faculty was truly a symptom of a very serious disease.

During one of our last bargaining sessions, the faculty team asked whether the dean of architecture had discussed this significant change with his faculty. Laughter ensued when it became clear that the dean had not and had chosen not to because the notion of raising the workload of a faculty obviously would not go over very well.

The dean's failure to share with faculty what he knew the administration was seeking to do was not the only example of feckless leadership he had exhibited, but it was among the most memorable for many of us. All union leaders will likely encounter similar "leaders," wherever they may be. Don't assume that their faculty have any idea what has been proposed by a given dean, because the dean may very well simply have cowered rather than led.

The reality is this: the inability to have difficult discussions in which rational decision making might be influenced by a variety of viewpoints simply doesn't exist at all, or perhaps even most, universities. If something positive can come out of the adversarial process of collective bargaining, perhaps it might center on addressing that real and fundamental flaw in our decision-making process. Is it any wonder that faculty distrust administration?

If there is a sincere desire to improve this model, then discussions between deans and faculty should take place far before proposals significantly impacting faculty are brought to the bargaining table. You might consider suggestions at your university for improving any similar process so that deans and faculty might be able to genuinely improve their respective schools by engaging in a genuinely collaborative thought process. Making those decisions at the bargaining table rather than in academic discussions is truly dysfunctional, and in fact, it would be difficult to imagine a worse method of decision making.

All of this seems similar to corporate decisions made in downsizing customer service. We are all now too familiar with the inability to talk to a real human being when dealing with a problem with our cell phone, or cable, or some other service to which we subscribe. Generally, we must endure a series of robo questions, and then after being told how much we are valued, we are put on hold to await a person who will assist us. That person, if unable to assist us, will put us on hold again to await a supervisor, and so on. We all know the drill, and we all know that the goal is to get the customer to hang up and go away. And thus, the corporation has won yet again.

At many universities, it would seem as though the goal of the university administration is simply to get us to "hang up." That our morale should be destroyed in the process matters little or perhaps not at all, so long as short-term concessions are granted and the board of trustees can be assured that the inmates are not running the asylum. And what an asylum it has become.

Rather than sully the administrative day with questions and academic discussion and efforts to improve the enterprise, we are encouraged to keep our thoughts to ourselves and move the assembly line forward. Perhaps a better analogy might be found in *One Flew over the Cuckoo's Nest*, where the inmates are given their medication and those in charge hope against hope that doing so will shut them up and allow the place to function in whatever unhealthy fashion that function takes.

This inability to agree about almost anything clearly illustrated that our research, our students' apparent fondness for us, our contributions to the community, and the reputation of the school were, in a word, irrelevant.

What mattered was that the administration viewed us as underworked and overpaid. Period. End of story.

If that sounds like a fairly poisonous negotiating environment, then it's been accurately portrayed in these pages. Eventually, of course, we came to terms. It would be impossible to objectively view those terms as particularly successful for the faculty, but recent history at our university has come to be more about stemming the corporate tide than achieving real and lasting victory or peace.

Until the faculty could truly come together and use the leverage they collectively had, rather than focus on narrow self-interest, they could never do more than merely slow the encroachment of the administration. Concessions seem to be made by the faculty with each ensuing contract, but any rage that might lead to collective action soon dissipates. And we all go back to minding our own business.

LESSONS LEARNED

When it comes to negotiating, there is truly no substitute for a hard and fast deadline. Though it's not as if that were a new discovery, you may nevertheless naïvely believe that an early start would lessen pressure on both sides and create a more civil and reasonable atmosphere, leading to a more favorable result. Not true. Absent a deadline, nothing really gets done. There's always tomorrow or next week; there's never a reason to compromise because there's always tomorrow or next week.

Don't assume that a department or group of faculty has been told what the administration intends to do "for" or "to" them. Even when it seems like a given dean or program director must surely have informed those under his or her charge that major changes are being considered and they should weigh in if they want to be heard, it simply isn't always the case. Sometimes, in fact, you may be shocked to learn that major programmatic changes advocated by a dean or at least accepted by a dean in the face of administrative pressure have not been shared with the faculty at all.

If you don't inform your faculty colleagues and major changes occur, it is very possible that those adversely affected will actually believe the union was a force behind the changes. Perhaps you didn't need this book to tell you "not to assume things," but truly, "don't assume things."

Another valuable if altogether trite lesson is: be true to yourself. Surround yourself with the people you believe will best serve the union. If possible, find at least one person you can trust who will put up with you in the worst of times. This cannot be emphasized enough because negotiations as a process can make you question yourself in ways that you may never have done before.

Don't succumb to the pressures of those who believe certain people must or must not serve on the negotiating committee. Do your best to trust your instincts, as difficult as that will be. You got elected to represent people, after all, so there should be some solace in the knowledge that if people were uncomfortable with your representation, they shouldn't have chosen you to represent them.

Obviously, you cannot please all the people all the time. And doing that which you truly believe is right is the only way you can sleep at night when you know (and you will come to know) that some of those you represent, many of whom may have even voted for you, are no longer supportive of your efforts. Your mother and grandmother were right all along: "All we can ask is that you do the best you can, and if you do that, there's absolutely nothing to be sorry about."

REFERENCES

Fish, S. (2008). *Save the World on Your Own Time*. New York: Oxford University Press.
Giroux, H. A. (2012). *Education and the Crisis of Public Values: Challenging the Assault on Teachers, Students, and Public Education*. New York: Peter Lang Publishing.

Chapter Twelve

The Slow but Sure Recovery of Your Mental Health

Professors face a complex choice: whether in addition to their classroom teaching, research agendas, and mostly mundane committee obligations, they will attempt to influence the greater university. Choosing to influence students beyond the classroom and/or choosing to influence university policies outside of the immediate department comes with risk.

It is surely a risk to devote time to something that may not bear fruit, particularly in a culture in which tangible evidence of "scholarship" is valued. Still, as professors, most of us view it to be part of our lives in academia to become an owner and investor in the university, rather than mere tenants (Barth, 2001). After all, most of us have already been on campus longer than any student, and we plan on being on campus longer still. For union activists, this choice can sometimes be even more difficult than it might be for those who tend to watch from the sidelines. Union activists, after all, are by their nature "activists," not "inactivists."

We all want our universities to be the best places they can be and the best environment in which we can reside. This could be altruism, but it can also simply be a desire to surround ourselves with better outcomes and less anguish from day to day.

We all want our campuses to be better places after we spend years on them than they were when we arrived. We cannot merely be a spectator and expect all of that "goodness" to come from somebody else, for we have a role to play in the success of our university, and we pride ourselves—usually, anyway—in attempting to play it with enthusiasm and professionalism.

After your presidency, your perspective may change, and it may be radically. You may now think Barth's words, useful as they were, had to have been written by someone who had had only positive experiences throughout his academic career. Serving as union president and then expecting to serve as a player in the "success" of the endeavor seems, in a word, ludicrous. Bridges are burned forever. Seeing the sausage being made and hearing the things that the administration says in "private" cannot be unseen and un-heard. Enthusiasm and professionalism take a backseat to survival and accep-tance. The party, once you've been union president, is over.

Perhaps such a statement should be tempered, for, after all, very few of us ever serve as union president at more than one university, and thus the vast majority of us deal with only one university administration in that capacity. Surely, there are administrations at universities in which the value placed upon collegiality and the faculty generally as a partner in the educational process allows for an entirely different experience than the one that has been described in these pages. Those types of collegial relationships must exist; they just don't exist for all of us and in all places.

Regaining one's equilibrium and emotional strength is probably not going to happen while one remains as union president. Only after your tenure as president ends will you fully be able to begin the long process of healing.

Although it may seem a bit dramatic, a lot of damage can and likely will be done. For some, it's not uncommon for your morale to be in the toilet and your sense of humor to be in disrepair.

Frankly, even driving through the gates and onto the campus brings a sense of foreboding for some long after their union presidency ends. Once you finally make your way into your office, you might find your door closed far more often than it is open, which for many of us reflects a significant departure from past practices of friendly banter with colleagues and students alike.

To get things to change in a healthy direction, there are a number of things that you'll have to let go. The notion of forgiveness is going to have to be very real. There will be people you genuinely felt had treated you poorly and unfairly, and some of those people were your friends. And if you are "big" enough to let it happen, they will be your friends again.

People you may have thought trusted you implicitly might not have trusted you as much as you may have thought. You may twist yourself into a pretzel making certain everything you do is completely transparent. There may be times when you desperately want to move things along by meeting individually with your adversary, but those who "trust" you don't necessarily seem to fully trust you to act on your own.

You may be consistently discouraged even by your negotiating team members and those outside of the team in whom you confide and in whom you'd come to depend. You must understand, after all, those on the team had sacrificed as much as you had and they deserved to be a part of all of it. If you truly understood that, you may never truly press the issue of individual meetings over any objections, though obviously, you have the power as the president to engage in them if you choose to do so.

It will seem at times as though there is nobody, not even those closest to you, who actually fully trusts you to do the right thing, or worse, they don't or won't trust that you are capable of fully understanding the implications of all that lies before you. It will bother you greatly, but in an effort to be a true team player and a true believer in the concept of full transparency with your team, you must avoid even the appearance of individual meetings, let alone any actual individual meetings.

In keeping with many of the themes of the preceding chapters, a person who serves in the role of union president will likely continue to struggle with many of the perceived injustices described in these pages. That struggle involves trying to reconcile one's own deficiencies with one's own sense of the deficiencies you might see in so many others involved in this process.

Why do so many of our union brothers and sisters seem to distrust us and the union more generally? What did we ever do to earn that distrust? Was it simply cumulative? Has there been so much damage done to the image of our union over the years that it is simply impossible for any single person to repair it? Beaten-down faculty syndrome?

There are so many vivid examples of administrative overreach and incompetence on so many university campuses that it would seem like all faculty members should have rushed to support their union and should have joined union officers in working tirelessly to ensure that some level of justice remained for all. Mostly, however, it was the usual course of events as reflected by a typical Bell curve.

A relatively few faculty members were involved and passionately working on improving the power of the union and the subsequent power and place of the faculty. A similarly relatively small number were simply anti-union. Some of those folks were just politically predisposed to dislike unions and unionism, and others in that group simply didn't believe the administration would ever do anything that wasn't in the workers' best interests.

The largest group—as usual, it would seem—was squarely in the middle and adept at straddling the fence. They were interested when contract negotiations were in full swing, and many had questions about how they individually would be affected by contractual provisions. But at other times, they simply didn't seem to care much about what the union was doing.

This Bell curve is always vividly illustrated in the attendance at union meetings. Attendance will likely involve a majority of faculty in the waning days of negotiations, when things are getting "interesting." But attendance in the off years, when a contract isn't being negotiated, will be slim. Only the very few continually "activist" union members will probably be bothered enough to show up. It didn't seem to matter how much notice a meeting would be given; it just wouldn't fit into the vast majority of faculty members' schedules when they didn't see a direct connection to their immediate concerns.

One could argue that such tales are evidence of selfishness when selflessness was needed. And in truth, that's probably in many ways inarguable, another example of "We have met the enemy, and the enemy is mostly us."

REFERENCE

Barth, R. (2001). *Learning by Heart*. San Francisco, CA: Jossey-Bass Publishers.

Chapter Thirteen

Mistakes Were Made

"Developing self-awareness is a lifelong process; you don't just wake up one day and have all you need." (Mastromonaco, 2017, p. 123)

As one's "representative" life continues to occupy inordinate amounts of your time, your actual professional life will march along with or without your full commitment and participation. You still have classes to teach, grades to compile, research to conduct, professional meetings to attend, and other duties to perform, as well as those it takes some effort to shirk. Among the things we all have to do is submit ourselves to student reviews and, the bane of many faculty members' existences, the self-compiled reviews required to achieve tenure and those required to maintain it.

One of the first titles that was considered for this book was *Mistakes Were Made*. Upon doing some research, however, it became clear that it was a title that had already been used. Like so many brilliant ideas, it took only a short while to realize that this "original" thought wasn't particularly original.

Representing one's colleagues isn't particularly original either, but the level of commitment necessary when serving as a union leader might very well prove to be a massive mistake for your personal and professional lives. Every mistake one makes representing others is magnified far beyond the mistakes one makes in representing only oneself. Even if others ultimately forgive those mistakes along the way, you may very well find it difficult to forgive yourself.

Having the willingness to stick one's neck out on behalf of your faculty colleagues inevitably means that, indeed, mistakes will be made along the way. Being active rather than passive means that risks will be taken and mistakes will occur. We learn the most from our mistakes, unfortunately; by the time we learn our lessons, it is usually too late for them to be used.

This book hopefully has been helpful in putting those lessons to practical use for those doing this sort of thing in the future. It's rather pointless to learn valuable lessons and then not use them or even share them. Many of you reading this have already served your time and won't be using them. But others of you are considering greater union involvement or are already on the battlefield, and for you, these lessons are here for the taking.

Most of us who become active in our unions are probably also active in other parts of campus life. When students ask us to attend a sporting event, we make every effort to be there. We attend dance concerts, student workshops, and a variety of things in which students are involved and take the lead, particularly when they ask us to follow.

Most of us see our participation in campus life as our duty, and the vast majority of the time, it's an easy and enjoyable duty. To various degrees, of course, we enjoy sports, we enjoy lively discussion, we enjoy the energy that comes from being around far younger people than ourselves. We enjoy participating in the life of the mind and in the vibrant life of our college campuses.

Clearly, the bulk of us want to improve the climate on our respective campuses. Some of us have worked tirelessly (until relatively recently when we just became too tired) in an effort to improve campus climate. Greater emphasis on integrity, diversity, and civility is a project that many of us have had a hand in on our own campuses.

Efforts of us older faculty are often buried in past history, as the present self-promotion available in a variety of social media forms often drowns out the "silent and growing older majority." Nevertheless, the historical reality on most campuses is that many of the "initiatives" of the present are firmly rooted in past practices. Many of us are involved in our workplaces and on campus as a matter of habit.

In *The Power of Habit*, Duhigg (2014) cites Geoffrey Hodgson and credits him with the quote "Routines are the organizational analogue of habits." Duhigg spent much of his best-selling book explaining how habits become entrenched in the lives of individuals as well as organizations.

At your university, it may seem as though much of what you do is about "habit" or "routine," for better or for worse. We involved ourselves in the many good things in the life of the university, and we simply did it the way we did it because that's the way we'd always done it. The futility of the process and the meaninglessness of the entire proceeding suggested that it was merely a part of the entrenched routine and little more.

To be fair, there are benefits to routines. "Among the most important benefits of routines is that they create truces between potentially warring groups or individuals within an organization" (Duhigg, 2014, p. 162). A truce between two warring groups aptly describes the situation in which union leaders may find themselves in almost all circumstances.

After negotiations end, it is possible if not probable that many members of the administration will hold you in contempt, and you may view them similarly. You may manage enough of a truce to get along with or at least not care about each other anymore and go on about your business without actively working to destroy each other. You may consider this an uneasy peace, but it is peace nonetheless.

The lack of a meaningful relationship between the rhetoric of the administration and the reality of how they actually view their faculty, at least at many institutions, seems wholly inconsistent with scholarship in the field. Some of that scholarship may even be touted by your own administration but then seemingly dismissed when the time comes to review a given professor's contributions on and off campus.

If the ongoing corporatization and de-academizing of the place were not enough (and frankly, it is quite enough), then there are the day-to-day oddities that make all of us question the wisdom of our decisions made long ago to enter graduate-degree programs and ultimately to pursue this "life of the mind." It's becoming the "life of the mind-less," as illustrated perhaps best by the many events that the university foists upon us to ostensibly improve a deteriorating workplace.

You may be offered workshops on civility or diversity or any number of important things meant to make you better people. There would be any number of more respectful ways to improve faculty and staff morale on a college campus without many of these demeaning programs, but this is where we find ourselves. It is likely not the intention of the administration to demean us through these programs, but the result remains the same.

Despite the mistakes you'll make, surely there will be good things done, advances made, and minor annoyances allayed. There must be occasional brushes with success that will leave a positive mark upon the union for those that follow. When your time as union president is finished, you will inevitably question your place and whether you've made a difference. Your activism suggests that you care, and the questioning you do of yourself will reflect that caring.

Ironically, many of the people you might consider most offensive with regard to their lack of caring about the collective generally and/or the union in particular may be those who clearly consider themselves "social activists." The key, it would seem, is that the social activism must come without personal risk. Although they'd support good union workers around the globe and post Facebook rantings about injustice and corporate domination worldwide, they were too weak to show their own faces at a union meeting where the president, provost, and their dean might get wind of their attendance or involvement and think less of them.

Their interest in union activities and the collective good did not extend beyond self-interest in their promotions and pay increases and how a contract covering hundreds would affect them and them alone. It may very well be, in a word, frustrating. In another word, it may be pathetic. "Social justice" without risk. "Me first" social justice. Pathetic.

It would be surprising if your campus didn't have similar characters, those quick to comment on national or world events and silent when it comes to campus events. "Think globally, not locally" would be the appropriate bumper sticker for their cars.

With experience, of course, comes wisdom. Wisdom, in many cases, takes far longer to achieve than it probably should. Given what has been said in these pages about the number of your colleagues who simply will not under any circumstances involve themselves in the union, it may be tempting to join them and simply "freeload" on the backs of the few who are willing to step up.

Those who step forward and at some risk to their own professional lives attempt to improve the professional lives of others are becoming increasingly rare. Working for the benefit of the whole sometimes runs directly counter to working for the benefit of the individual.

Despite any seeming nobility of working for the betterment of others, it's difficult to fully endorse the concept after one knows what is truly involved in representing one's peers as a university union leader. In fact, many of the most sensible people at the university seem to make an effort to avoid involvement in union activities. In essence, it seems absolutely right to endorse "the concept" of collectivism and social activism on behalf of your colleagues. Endorsing the actual "practice" of the same must be accompanied by a myriad of disclaimers, as the practice comes with risk.

It's difficult not to offer advice leaning toward union disengagement to those of you reading this who may be thinking of increased union activism. All of that work you are considering doing will likely never be rewarded and, in fact, may very likely cause you nothing but pain over the long haul.

Your colleagues will almost certainly be unappreciative of the work you do on their behalf, administrators may very well hold grudges, and all in all, your time on campus will never be the same. Another inarguable truism that sometimes takes years to grasp is simply that loyalty to the university is not likely to be reciprocated.

In an increasingly corporatized culture in which administrators have little or no academic experience, loyalty to the "cause" of academia may seem to be valueless. Many of us once believed that those doing good and even great things for the students, the university, and academia would be rewarded, nurtured, valued, and even protected. There is little tangible evidence to support such a belief.

On many campuses, if the very best of us would offer to leave so that younger and far cheaper replacements could be hired, such an exodus would be viewed by the administration not as a loss to the university community but as a massive economic victory for the administration. There is frequently no caring about the academic product (beyond the rhetoric, which is often truly spectacular).

It's a bottom-line business now in which widgets are mass-produced and the faculty are merely interchangeable cogs necessary to produce the revenue that allows overpaid administrators to keep replicating themselves. That assessment, of course, is not true everywhere.

There are places in which administrators support the good works of faculty and the mission of the university remains a full commitment to the educational process. Unfortunately, on many campuses, that ship has sailed long ago.

Perhaps on campuses with relatively low endowments it is even more likely that a more business-oriented perspective takes precedence over a more academic-minded model. Too many boards of trustees simply follow too long a history of a pro-business, anti-academia model of a bottom-line immediate rewards structure at the expense of forward-thinking planning and commitments.

But we expected the university administration to be difficult; our larger problem was our own membership. Most of our members couldn't be bothered by any level of involvement up to and including occasional attendance at a union meeting. Others seemed unconcerned about negotiations at all until, of course, the end game was nearing and they made the late determination that they had been betrayed by the negotiating team. Although most of the members couldn't have done less, there was always a belief that those who were working tirelessly on their behalf could have done more.

Clearly, we've met the enemy, and in many cases, the enemy is us. It was frustrating enough negotiating with a university administration seemingly unconcerned about any aspect of academia, from faculty morale to the increasing use of adjuncts. Any appeals about the culture of integrity on campus and the need to improve the academic climate were basically falling upon deaf ears, because the other side was concerned only about the economic bottom line.

Dependency on more and more adjuncts was not perceived to be a problem by the administration, and clearly in their "perfect world," we'd all be adjuncts. Any notion of lessening our dependence on adjuncts was intended only for the off-campus audience and, of course, visiting accreditation teams. In reality, there would be no real effort of going beyond the rhetoric employed.

At a meeting of the membership long after my presidency had ended and while my successor and friend stood at the lectern at the front of the large auditorium, a voice from the back of the room called out, "You always tell us we should be wary of the administration, but why should we trust you?" We proceeded as we so often did and still do by quietly ruminating about the insanity that was so pervasive within our own membership in an organization so loosely put together that calling it an organization was a disservice to that term.

"Why should we trust you?" Maybe because we are on "your side," maybe because we were elected by our peers, maybe because to not trust "us" means not trusting "yourselves." Maybe ultimately because to not trust us means you would be trusting the administration that has been working consistently to make you work longer hours for less pay and fewer benefits for several negotiating cycles now. Come to think of it, maybe we can't be trusted . . . any of us. What total absurdity. What total lunacy. We indeed have met the enemy, and the enemy is us.

If the enemy isn't us, it might be the representatives assigned to us by the national education organization that, on paper at least, are paid through our union dues to represent us. In each negotiation (negotiations that they used to lead for us, but which, in recent years, we've felt compelled to serve in as our own lead negotiators at the bargaining table), our "leaders" from outside the campus seemed to always take the side of the administration. "Times are tough, and the university is in dire financial straits; they aren't telling you anything that isn't true . . . take the offer."

If we had acted on our off-campus organization's advice, our increasingly inferior contracts would have been far worse than they have been. You may face a similarly "uninterested" national "support" system, at least uninterested insofar as seeing little or no need to put more time in on your behalf than you absolutely demand of them. You will find yourself absolutely demanding it, but you may also find yourself so unimpressed by their efforts that your demands will decrease, and eventually you'll find more solace in simply doing it yourself. It's hard to get good help . . . and all of that.

Many of us could point to any number of instances during our tenure as union presidents when we were advised to take what the other side was offering. Fortunately, most of us were unwilling to do so, and we were able to negotiate at least slightly better terms. Again, with friends like these, who really needs enemies?

> "As I now move, graciously, I hope, toward the door marked exit, it occurs to me that the only thing I ever really liked to do was go to the movies." (Vidal, 2006, p. 1)

> "I don't think anyone has ever found startling the notion that it is not *what* things are that matters so much as *how* they are perceived." (Vidal, 2006, p. 6)

Perhaps many of you reading this work have written a fair amount yourselves. If so, you've probably submitted a work for publication and have been made to answer the question "Who is your audience, what type of reader is your book intended to reach?" If you have read certain passages within and you've felt as though "you've been there" too, then this work has been of benefit to both of us, and it has reached the audience for which it was intended.

LESSONS LEARNED

Be prepared to defend your choices. People don't trust leaders who shrug off decisions and/or blame others for decisions they made or should've made. It's genuinely amazing how an air of confidence plays into success, even if it requires tremendous skill in acting. I've heard that basketball and football referees and baseball umpires are taught to make their calls with confidence. Letting others see your own doubts can be deadly. Obviously, educated people often doubt their every move because there are always possible choices to be made, but letting those you lead see you question your own leadership quite naturally leads to a rather general questioning of your leadership.

Satisfy yourself with doing the best you can given a variety of often hideous choices, but doing the best you can requires that you impress upon others that you are confident in the choices you make. Mastromonaco (2017) wrote, "One of the hallmarks of a great leader is being able to explain your decisions" (p. 17). She was writing about President Obama, but one doesn't need to be at that level to understand the need to be able to explain your decisions.

Frankly, it's pretty simple; it's difficult to appear confident in your decision making if you cannot even explain why you made a given decision. So understand the issue, make the decision, and explain it to those who ask; then, be prepared someday to explain it to those who didn't ask at the time.

For those of you starting out in academia, the obvious needs to be restated: concentrate on those things that will get you tenure (provided, of course, that tenure still exists at your institution). Publishing, even if you are not at a publish-or-perish type of place, is incredibly important and will garner you lasting professional capital.

Those other things, like good teaching, good advising, quality mentorship, community service, and the like, although critical to your own personal and professional success, are far less valued by those above you (and even beside you) who will be making those tenure decisions. Your publishing and research record will stand out, or not. It is as close to an objective measure that you can create for yourself.

Your teaching record, in contrast, is almost purely subjective; students will like you and possibly even hate you largely depending on what grades you distribute, and you can likely produce evidence of that very thing. Those professors who award excellent grades tend to be liked. Those who don't, tend to be loathed. It's unfortunate that it is that simple for most of our student populations, but it's that simple. Despite the rhetorical value that is placed upon teaching evaluations, the reality is that good ones are undervalued and diminished and bad ones are largely attributed to factors outside of your teaching abilities.

REFERENCES

Duhigg, C. (2014). *The Power of Habit: Why We Do What We Do in Life and Business*. New York: Random House Publishers.

Mastromonaco, A. (2017). *Who Thought This Was a Good Idea? And Other Questions You Should Have Answers to When You Work in the White House*. New York: Twelve Books.

Vidal, G. (2006). *Point to Point Navigation: A Memoir*. New York: Doubleday.

Afterthoughts

A Lesser Man's Search for a Lesser Meaning

It is possible, maybe even likely, that many of you who chose to read a book like this are already struggling with a search for meaning concerning aspects of your own working lives. Perhaps you may even be familiar with Victor Frankl's (1984) classic *Man's Search for Meaning*, in which the renowned psychologist and concentration camp survivor suggests that the search for happiness can happen only when you stop caring about it so much. "Success, like happiness, cannot be pursued; it must ensue, and it only does so as the unintended side-effect of one's personal dedication to a cause greater than oneself as the by-product of one's surrender to a person other than oneself" (p. 17).

Frankl lived through hell and obviously came out the other side with an accumulation of wisdom that most never attain. The very idea of concentration camps and surviving one's experience within a concentration camp is beyond the reach of most of us. Thankfully, for those of us reading these words, our "experiences" with these horrors are limited to a visit to the Holocaust Museum in Washington, DC, or possibly a trip visiting the grounds of Auschwitz or Dachau.

Understanding that the reality of visiting a museum or a sacred place where atrocities occurred is far removed from the actual experience, such visits nevertheless tend to leave the visitors profoundly moved if not entirely shaken to their foundations. Such visits should probably impress upon all that our own "suffering" belongs in quotation marks because it doesn't compare to the very real suffering that has occurred in this world historically, suffering that tragically continues in certain corners of the globe, far removed for the most part from the place in which those of you reading this are now sitting.

The appreciation of this reality makes writing a book about one's place and one's frustration with that place necessarily rather unimportant when that place involves a level of human comfort that those who really suffer could not imagine in their wildest dreams. So my own search for meaning is a vastly lesser man's search for a vastly lesser meaning. Perhaps that should've been mentioned in the preface rather than the afterthoughts, but it seemed like too much of a downer. Instead, acknowledging this reality may fit better at or near the end of people's reflection of their own place in the universe and their own place in the much smaller universe of their workplace.

Many of our colleagues on college and university campuses across America often share the dark humor that surrounds the notion that no matter how bad things become, they can always be worse. Always. Even in our comfortable environment, in which we worry about mundane things rather than life and death and about mostly unintentional slights rather than intentional cruelty, we nevertheless find ourselves worrying and suffering in our own comparatively meaningless ways.

Should we be encouraged by the notion that things can always get worse? If history is our judge, then things not only can get worse, but in higher education in recent years, they mostly have gotten worse.

On most of our own campuses when people come and go and policies change accordingly, things have indeed gotten worse; but on the bright side, they aren't as bad as they could be or someday might be. Perhaps this isn't about one lesser man's search for a lesser meaning, but in some ways, it's a lesser man's search for complete meaninglessness.

Searching for meaning has been difficult and is elusive for most of us in the end, but the search for meaninglessness, in many of our present environments, can be as easy as falling out of bed. It just happens without effort. As Frankl suggested so long ago, stopping the search is the only way to find what one is actually seeking.

Frankl also wrote of what he witnessed in the concentration camps with regard to his comrades: "Some . . . behave like swine while others behaved like saints. Man has both potentialities within himself; which one is actualized depends on decisions but not on conditions" (p. 157). Unionism offers a chance for people to step up and work on behalf of others, just as it offers many of those others the chance to avoid responsibility at all costs.

What about all the good things? There are plenty of good people at our universities, the "saints" among the "swine." Thousands of them, probably. There are professors who give of their own time and often their own money to try to improve the lives of their students. There are students who believe in the institution and who take pride in the place in hopes that their degrees will become more meaningful and their educational experiences, as well as their experiences on campus more generally, will have been truly productive.

Those are the things that are supposed to be normal, and those are the things that are rather normal at campuses across the land. "Normal" isn't newsworthy, and why would it be? When normal, in contrast, becomes newsworthy, then abnormal becomes the norm.

The concept of the normal becoming the newsworthy and the abnormal becoming the norm first came to my attention in LeDuff's (2013) book about his hometown of Detroit, titled, perhaps not surprisingly, *Detroit*. LeDuff pointed out so many problems facing his hometown and the city to which he returned after many years away that part of the "problem" was that problems were now the norm.

In essence, things were so entirely messed up that people were no longer surprised when terrible things happened and that the previously inexplicable was now subject to explanation or, worse, acceptance. We must do all we can to make sure that universities don't become so entirely messed up that we are no longer surprised when terrible things happen.

All that said, as you near the end of this book, I hope that you have found that this story has been worth telling. Even if people have not been clamoring for it to be told, it's compelling enough to be told. Much of the need to tell it lies in making sure that we simply don't accept what shouldn't be acceptable. If we cannot change those things we'd so like to change, at least we can write about the structural problems inherent on many campuses and warn others about those things that need our attention. To do nothing is to whistle past the graveyard or to deny the leaking roof above our heads.

Shouldn't our expectations be a bit higher? Is what we see all around us truly what passes for "leadership" in twenty-first-century America? What can we do aside from writing about it and encouraging all to actually think about what they are seeing play out before them? Forget the death of expertise; we may be witnessing the death of competence.

Teaching has been given such bad press that it hardly seems defensible any longer, even though as a profession it should absolutely be defended. Maybe it's like every other profession in the sense that it's not that difficult to do something poorly but it is very difficult and impossible for most to do something really well.

We all want our students to remember us not just as their teachers but as teachers who taught them well. If that can be our legacy, then all the rest of it professionally was just all the rest of it, nothing more. So in defense of all of us who teach our students and try to do it well, we try because we still care about trying to be good at a profession that has value. In contrast, most of those above us in our university hierarchies don't seem to care whether we are doing our jobs well. In spite of all of it, we persist. That speaks very well of our collective character and very well of the profession.

Most of us never anticipated that serving as union president would transform us into festering boils of equal parts malice, resentment, and hopelessness. We may have expected certain things, but not that, or at least not all of that. Perhaps if we had to do it all over again, we'd do things differently.

Actually, if many of us had the chance to do things all over again, there's no way we'd do the same or even similar things all over again. In essence, although mistakes would still be made, fewer of them would be made if we had a second chance.

For many of us who served our union colleagues as presidents of our faculty unions, there are times when those entire chapters of our lives would be erased. If we could do it all over again, many of us would have simply continued on an easier path toward likeability and respectability and far less union activism.

Many of us, maybe most of us, surely wouldn't have subjected ourselves to that which we have subjected ourselves. We certainly wouldn't have spent our own social, cultural, and political capital on people who (mostly, at least) wouldn't consider doing the same for us (or anyone). But then again, people who are active and believe in the virtue of collective action perhaps cannot save themselves from themselves.

With the benefit of hindsight, a person can truly sit back, reflect, and consider the cast of characters that has assembled before them over the years. In the university setting, that typically means sharing the company of some of the most intelligent and hard-working people you could ever hope to encounter and some of the most reprehensible bottom-feeders you could ever imagine. You will work with people of great integrity, honor, and decency, as well as those with whom those words weren't even passing acquaintances. You will see it all, you will hear it all, and much of it you still will not believe.

There will be true profiles in courage, paralleled unfortunately by studies in spinelessness that would make any invertebrate proud. Thankfully, and most importantly, by the time this is published, my own memories of these experiences will have inevitably faded and been replaced (hopefully) by more pleasant recollections more consistent with better mental health.

My wish is for these stories to bear some fruit for the readers who may be contemplating the acceptance of a thankless position of leadership and for those around them to advise them wisely. Truly, who would want a virtually unpaid presidency? Looking back, it's almost incomprehensible to imagine such a decision being based on anything other than entirely misplaced hubris and entirely unrealistic expectations. Some decisions are simply worse than others.

One doesn't have to be a union president to understand that the coupling of high self-esteem and little real knowledge makes for a fairly miserable outcome. Such a combination can be deadly in a variety of circumstances, and most certainly it can seem deadly in a leadership position. Know thyself.

Know those around you whom you care about, and share this with them if they are contemplating taking on unpaid (or poorly paid) positions of leadership in their organizations. Maybe they really can make their world a better world, and more power to those who can. Just be careful out there; it's even potentially worse than you can imagine.

It would be impossible in one relatively brief afterword to adequately convey the disappointment you may potentially experience during your own negotiations. That disappointment may run the gamut, from deteriorating personal perceptions of the administrators who work as your foes at the bargaining table to your own faculty, whose collective shrug in the face of adversity will lay the groundwork for a series of ever-worsening contracts. The phrase "We are our own worst enemies" is entirely applicable to most faculty unions.

Given the profound differences present on all university faculties, the likelihood that you might face a similarly disjointed collection of individuals is high. Instead of coming together in the face of administrative attacks, you may very well fracture into splinter groups so self-interested that it becomes impossible to see any type of a forest through the trees.

So many individuals want so many individual benefits, some of which may be almost entirely idiosyncratic, that it often simply becomes impossible to talk about negotiations. Even discussions in the abstract may deteriorate almost immediately into "How does this affect me?" Any response bordering on "look at the big picture" or "this is about the collective good" might just as well be spoken in Swahili. Remarkably, few people could understand such a language, and most had zero interest in learning how to understand it.

What will likely be most frustrating with regard to so many of your colleagues on the faculty is their sheer self-interest and unabashed cowardice when it comes to facing down any challenges that you might face. Most faculty will be quite content for you and your negotiating team to take stands, to do whatever it might take on their behalf and risk your own political and social capital, but few will be willing to show any support publicly.

At our university, polling was done to assess the faculty's willingness to engage in potential workplace job actions. You will not be surprised, given what has already been said in these pages, that the numbers showed some truly discouraging things with regard to the place of collective action and sentiment within the university setting. Around 20 percent of the faculty surveyed suggested that they'd be willing to engage in "informational leafletting," something the faculty union leadership viewed as rather easy to swallow. After all, it wasn't striking; it wasn't even picketing. It doesn't take a beautiful mind to understand that such a number suggests that 80 percent of faculty wouldn't be willing to do even that.

Perhaps the statistic that most clearly illustrates the frustration faced by union leadership in the university setting is this: although only 20 percent of the faculty would themselves be willing to engage in informational leafletting, fully 80 percent of the faculty would support the negotiating team engaging in such activity. Once again, the faculty at large seems to be saying to the leadership, "Get out there, work on our behalf, take risks for yourselves personally and professionally, and we're right behind you as long as absolutely no risk accrues to us."

During the next negotiation period, four years after the completion of the negotiations mostly referred to herein, our union president asked faculty members to wear buttons proclaiming their membership in the union. The buttons didn't say anything controversial; they were even thoughtfully ordered with magnetic backings so as not to damage clothing upon which they might be worn, and yet the number of members who wore them was relatively miniscule.

Most, all too willing to criticize, all too willing to expect the negotiating team to do everything in their power and to spend all time and effort necessary to provide for the best interests of the membership, couldn't be bothered to wear buttons illustrating union unity. They wouldn't want the administration to think of them negatively, after all. All of that negativity would have to be borne by the union president and the negotiating team. They could set their own futures on fire, no need for the rank and file to diffuse any of the heat.

It can be infuriating for a union leader, and it can remain infuriating years later. At the time, after all, you could at least blame yourself for some of the failings of the collective and for the failure to unify faculty. Years later, it may make you even angrier to see through clearer eyes the full display of naked self-interest.

"Friendly fire" from inside the faculty is dangerous, but the reason inside sniping is so utterly frustrating is because it shouldn't have to be that way. There is a clear common "enemy," and it takes remarkably little interaction with the administration to recognize clearly drawn battle lines. The administration is determined, understandably, to please the trustees above all else, and shielding the trustees from what actually happens on campus is often a major role of a university president and his or her trusted advisors.

It's frequently the case that nothing can permeate the bubble that surrounds the inner circle of high-ranking administrators and the board of trustees, the ultimate parallel universe in which those on the inside are convinced that those on the outside offer nothing of value. Or so it seemed to those of us on the outside—but then again, we were on the outside.

It seemed a lot cozier on the inside, and although you might get occasional glimpses into the finances of the university, and you can do your best to demand as much information as you can, there will still be a significant level of secrecy and a lack of transparency. Given that level of secrecy, it's almost impossible to truly feel fully prepared when it comes to making comparisons and appeals regarding inequitable treatment. Not that appeals relating to inequitable treatment hold much sway in corporatized academia, where those at the top believe they need great incentives to do great things and those at the bottom are viewed as workers always able to do more with less. Even if success is unlikely, due diligence nevertheless requires that you make your very best efforts to get as much information as you possibly can.

In most instances, those involved in the negotiations will sign some form of an agreement not to unilaterally involve the press during the course of the negotiations. It seems only fair. You might also consider including some players on the periphery within that agreement.

Many times, for example, although your university's president may not be a party to the negotiations, he or she will obviously be informed of the progress. The president's sharing "inside" information with the media, particularly with the student newspaper, can be damaging given that any representations made, true or not, are difficult to ethically rebut. Including in the agreement that the president, deans, and other cabinet-level officials not speak of the process and progress of ongoing negotiations is advice that all union presidents should heed.

Once a contract has been voted on by the faculty, it may perhaps be appropriate to inform the students of the process with a bit more detail than they might have previously been given. Although it would not be appropriate for a union president to share specific statements made at the negotiating table during the course of many months, it would perhaps be appropriate to share the tenor of the negotiations so that students and the campus community may better understand the "culture."

Every university has a culture. Most university cultures consist of largely positive environments in which living and learning thrive and working relationships between and among staff, students, faculty, and administration align or mostly align to create positive experiences for all members of the university community.

That said, no university is free from shocks to the system that confront the many good things that occur on a daily basis. Penn State no doubt continues to confront the shock to its culture that saw its students, alumnae, faculty, and staff embarrassed over scandals in which the vast majority of them had no input or control. Harvard confronted a scandal in its athletic department that caused that community much embarrassment and consternation. The University of North Carolina saw widespread cheating overtake a portion of its athletic community, which played out in newspapers across the country. As this is written, Michigan State is still reeling from the reprehensible misconduct of a person in a position of trust.

Although contract negotiations generally do not rock the foundation of a university, there are tremors from that process that might result in some lesser aftershocks that may potentially alter the "culture" of the university for many years. For those involved in the negotiations, they may personally change some of their views about the "partnership" rhetoric that they likely hear at public ceremonies. The very notion that your university is an institution committed to improving the standing of all who enter it might very well take a bit of a hit.

One's belief that university administration has a genuine interest in shepherding the university forward positively so that each person within the university is enhanced by making the degrees your students attain seem more valuable, your teaching better, and your research appear more worthwhile may take a hit. Perhaps the administration as guided by the board of trustees really does put students first and values the faculty as professionals assigned to mentor and monitor and truly educate the "whole person," but that belief might also take a hit.

The university is increasingly a corporate culture, one in which those at the top are rewarded handsomely and those at the bottom are "incentivized" to work harder with less. The faculty are somewhere in between. Nobody would suggest that faculty are struggling economically in the same way that many staff people are. Those folks, from our unionized secretaries to our unionized food service workers and maintenance personnel, have suffered far greater financial hits than the faculty have. We have taken these hits not because our universities have always needed us to take them, but because our universities have been able to hit us in their ongoing efforts to distinguish ever more clearly between the administration and everyone else: the "workers."

William Chace, a former president of Emory and Wesleyan, wrote *100 Semesters: My Adventures as a Student, Professor, and University President, and What I Learned along the Way*. All should be encouraged to read Chace's account of his experiences, and university administrators would particularly benefit from a consideration of it. Chace referred to faculty as "not so much the employees of the institution as they are its intellectual engine and its most important asset. They are 'capital' rather than 'labor'" (2006, p. 224).

The thought of faculty as capital rather than labor is often the opposite of the approach taken during negotiations. During negotiations, in contrast, you might find the administration desiring that all "labor" be treated the same and all labor to be dismissed as far more fungible than it might actually be.

"A university is not a business" (Chace 2006, p. 234), but it certainly seems like one in many places. That may be due to the fact that most trustees have a business emphasis in the vast majority of their professional lives that dictates their way of thinking, to our long-term detriment. It would be impossible to truly express the magnitude of the administration's desire to "treat all labor the same" and the damage that does to a faculty who are far from treated as valuable capital of the institution (except, of course, rhetorically to our faces at the beginning and end of the school year).

On most college and university campuses, the corporatization of the university continues, and faculty morale has correspondingly deteriorated. Most importantly, perhaps, there is no indication that the majority of university presidents actually care about fractured relationships or fractured morale; it's simply not important in an increasingly corporate workplace.

All workers become fungible, including professors. Tenure-track lines are being diminished as term lecturer positions enter the university. What the faculty face in this not-so-brave new world are simply the logical conclusions of a corporate mentality that has fully engulfed the administrative buildings. Many of these administrative buildings no longer contain former faculty members who had chosen the administrative path. Instead, they are becoming populated with career administrators who seem little interested in what happens in the classrooms, beyond keeping all students happy and paying tuition.

Chace (2006, p. 319) chided his own trustees for their mistaken notions that the president should be treated like a CEO rather than as an intellectual and a moral leader, and of course, that meant that he should be compensated like a CEO too. It is difficult for faculty members to endure the talk of "tough times" coming from the other side while you are privy to the reality that many of their salaries and certainly the salary of our leaders are many times that of most of the membership.

Many critics contend that just because corporate America engages in excessive greed is no reason for a private university to go down that same road. Nobody argues that the president should be our highest paid official . . . but really . . . must the president be paid approximately five or more times as much as the average professor? Is that the type of fiscal responsibility that your trustees apparently value at the expense of your intellectual capital? Are you merely labor after all, and thus should your opinions be muted rather than heard and considered as voices necessary to improve the functioning of the academic enterprise?

It's not as if "fairness" isn't understood by the administration during negotiations. They will likely make quite a point of making sure "in the interest of fairness" that every employee on campus contributes the same toward his or her health care, despite repeated requests that they might consider the different circumstances of those making five-figure incomes versus the very different circumstances of most of our presidents and high-ranking administrators. It would seem that even agreement on what "fairness" actually means would be impossible.

It is difficult to be upbeat when you feel the work you do is underappreciated and the enterprise of which you are a part fails to share the values you do. Frankly, it may very well seem as though the only values the university has are the common corporate values of low overhead and cost-effectiveness.

Seeing employee morale as simply unimportant to the success of the venture seems to be the new normal among many administrative teams. It seems surprising that more administrators do not or cannot understand that their workers' work product and devotion to the cause could be enhanced through a more respectful workplace. It often seems as though many of those at the top of the organization know nothing about organizational theory and workplace efficiency. It's weird; it really is.

The character of your university's administration can be determined through considering whether there is a match between their rhetoric and their practices or whether there seems to frequently be a complete disconnect between their words and their actions. If they frequently speak of the "full partnership" with faculty but then are never truthful with their full partners, then you'll know how meaningless words can really be. Is the financial condition of your university presented one way to the public and another completely different way to the faculty and staff?

A lack of involvement on campus is the product of an administration uninterested in improving academic performance or academic culture or valuing the time of its faculty. Doing "enough" is almost always good enough in many workplace cultures, and sadly, many academic places are no different. In some cases, in fact, doing enough is often doing too much. Staying silent and on the sidelines is the way to advance, and most of us play the game well enough to advance ourselves accordingly. The disincentive to stick one's neck out is great, and most people adhere to it.

A workplace culture has been created in which many of us do what is expected of us and sometimes very little more because the reward for "doing the right thing" isn't any greater than so vividly "doing the wrong thing." An argument could be made that doing the right thing is actually closer to professional suicide than shutting one's eyes and seeing no harm, and it would be an argument that many would find compelling.

The poisonous culture is represented in a variety of ways, and it seems so obvious at every public event in which administrators and faculty are represented that it almost becomes painful to endure. There are so many stories that seem to express the separation between the faculty and administration that several books could be written from a purely anecdotal perspective.

One overarching theme that seems to transcend the years and continues to be a significant factor in each and every new negotiation is the seeming inability of the administration to grasp why or how it might be possible that many if not most faculty members simply don't trust them. Accepting that one can always find bootlickers, who do indeed trust those above them in any organization despite all evidence suggesting that they shouldn't, overall, there is a pervasive sense of distrust borne out over many years of dishonesty.

After having been lied to over and over for decades, many faculty members have honed their already fairly impressive levels of cynicism. Each time a new negotiation cycle begins, the administration's negotiators may predictably express their amazement and befuddlement that there is such an atmosphere of distrust. In response, the faculty negotiator explains, as best he or she can, that many instances of dishonesty tend to breed an atmosphere in which things that are said are not always immediately accepted as true.

Many of us on the faculty remain unduly optimistic that we can be better people and that we can continue to expect better things of ourselves. Most of us harbor no such illusions about our administrations. They are who they are, as they say. Expect no better. All of which leads to a closing thought concerning expectations.

The expectation for this book is that it serves as something more than an irresponsible attack on administrations. Hopefully, it serves a more useful and edifying purpose: to better inform a shrinking professoriate of the value in resistance and the usefulness inherent in trying to find a better way despite the many trials and tribulations you will endure along the way.

LESSONS LEARNED

As I was finishing this book, I was reading an outstanding book titled *Who Thought This Was a Good Idea?* In it, Alyssa Mastromonaco (2017) details her experiences serving as President Obama's deputy chief of staff. A pretty heady position and a pretty damn good title for a book (further proof, as if we needed it, that most of the very best ideas and titles have already been taken). Anyway, the book is terrific, funny, interesting, and well written.

Mastromonaco answers the question that many of us have about people who find themselves in really significant positions: "How could someone like you end up in a job like that?" Her answer is deceptively simple. "Hard work and a good attitude can get you further than you could ever dream" (p. 6). Better career advice can truly not be given . . . work hard, smile when you can, laugh when appropriate (and privately even when it's not), and be kind to others. It's all your mother would ever ask of you, and none of us should probably ask for more.

REFERENCES

Chace, W. M. (2006). *100 Semesters: My Adventures as Student, Professor, and University President, and What I Learned along the Way*. Princeton, NJ: Princeton University Press.
Frankl, V. (1984). *Man's Search for Meaning*. New York: Simon & Schuster.
LeDuff, C. (2013). *Detroit: An American Autopsy*. New York: Penguin Books.

Mastromonaco, A. (2017). *Who Thought This Was a Good Idea? And Other Questions You Should Have Answers to When You Work in the White House.* New York: Hatchette Book Group.

Index

About the Author

Robert Engvall is a professor of Justice Studies at Roger Williams University in Bristol, Rhode Island, where he has taught since 1999. He has written numerous books and articles on topics ranging from collective bargaining to identity politics in education.

www.ingramcontent.com/pod-product-compliance
Lightning Source LLC
Chambersburg PA
CBHW020356270326
41926CB00007B/467